ADVANCE PRAISE

"Common sense about marketing in uncommonly well-told examples. Atul Minocha has lived it, and you would be wise to go on his journey of experience and wisdom."

—CHUCK ALVEY, VISTAGE CHAIR

"Taking a 'forest' view and working with the 'trees' in this business jungle is what Atul does best. He used his framework and principles to help us grow 6x in five years and get acquired by a large services company in 2020. The same methodical and logical approach is reflected in this must-read book for CEOs and business owners."

—ANURAG KUMAR, FOUNDER AND CEO, ITEXICO (AN IMPROVING COMPANY)

"Real-world experience trumps long-standing myths to create a much-needed pragmatic CEO's guide to getting the most from marketing. Easy read with thoughtful analysis and examples."

—DAN KERPELMAN, PRESIDENT AND CEO, BIO-OPTRONICS INC.

"In the work that Atul did for our company, I learned many of the lessons he elucidates in Lies, Damned Lies, and Marketing. It reminded me why his approach was so effective: he asks the right questions and distills complex systems into clear, actionable ideas."

—MOLLY KELLOGG, CEO, HUBBARD-HALL INC.

"Chock-full of great advice from an experienced CMO who is passionate about helping companies make sense of their marketing. At Rösler, we worked with Atul and implemented many of the recommendations he outlines in his new book. And we see the impact on our business. Thanks for providing this 'manual' with a lot of practical advice."

—BERNIE KERSCHBAUM, CEO,
RÖSLER METAL FINISHING USA

"In this book, Atul reveals at least a dozen lies that have been served by marketing agencies. I know of no better way to learn the truth about marketing and reap its benefits. Invaluable!"

—PATRICK RENVOISE, PRESIDENT, SALES BRAIN, LLC;
CO-AUTHOR OF THE PERSUASION CODE

"Atul does a wonderful job of breaking down marketing into small, bite-sized areas of improvement which allow you to quickly alter your marketing strategy and the impact it has by attacking the area that needs improvement. All this without all the fluff!"

—STEPHEN BLANCHARD, COO, TRIO ELECTRIC, LLC

"Sharp and simple insights from years of practical experience are succinctly put and illustrated contextually—making this an extremely relevant read for anyone wanting to get more out of their marketing."

"Atul Minocha has written the best strategic and 'how-to' marketing book for small and midsize businesses I have read. The book captures the marketing dilemmas faced by company CEOs and provides marketing strategies and tactics for creating and maintaining a long-term, successful marketing approach."

"Through this book, Atul has brought together his rich experience across multiple decades, from starting off as an 'accidental marketer' to working with multinational companies globally, practicing the art and science of marketing. Filled with real-life experiences and anecdotes, this book demystifies the world of marketing in an ever-changing world moving from brick and mortar to mouse clicks and mobile. It will definitely help CEOs and other C-level executives leverage the new-age marketing tools while avoiding many common pitfalls. Excellent read from an accomplished practitioner."

LIES, DAMNED LIES, AND MARKETING

SEPARATE FACT FROM FICTION and DRIVE GROWTH

ATUL V. MINOCHA

LIONCREST
PUBLISHING

LIES, DAMNED LIES, AND MARKETING
Separate Fact from Fiction and Drive Growth

ISBN   978-1-5445-2123-7 *Hardcover*
　　　　978-1-5445-2122-0 *Paperback*
　　　　978-1-5445-2121-3 *Ebook*
　　　　978-1-5445-2199-2 *Audiobook*

To my mother,
who gave me the instinct to discern lies,
and to my father who, unbeknownst to me,
developed my love for marketing
by sharing his love for economics.

CONTENTS

INTRODUCTION

Has your marketing team ever left you feeling disappointed? Maybe they made promises that they didn't or couldn't keep, or worse, maybe it seems like they willfully misled and lied to you.

Of course you've felt like this. I'm guessing it's, at least in part, why you're reading this book.

Like most CEOs and business leaders, you've probably been burned by bad experiences with marketing. Maybe you've begun to suspect that your chief marketing officer (CMO) and the marketing team have been taking you for a ride with their "lies and damned lies" (as Mark Twain might have put it). As a result, you might even be wondering if you should simply avoid the problem altogether by eliminating, or at least minimizing, the role of marketing.

If you've felt this way, you are not alone in questioning the value of marketing. Let's suppose you're in a boat with your entire C-suite, and the boat starts to sink. To stay afloat, you realize you'll have to throw someone overboard. Who's going first? Certainly not the CFO. You'll keep the CFO to the bitter end. No, chances are, the CMO is getting tossed before anyone else. "Good luck, buddy. Hope you can swim!" If someone has to go overboard, it might as well be the person whose contribution is unclear.

While this frustration is common, you can't just abandon marketing because of bad experiences or disappointing results. That's like saying, "I got shampoo in my eyes, and it really stung. So, I no longer believe washing my hair is good for me." Marketing can't—and shouldn't—be avoided. Doing so will only lead to a whole host of problems and significant underperformance.

Every year, a New York-based market intelligence and business analytics company, named CB Insights, conducts a study of private companies that have closed shop in the previous twelve months, analyzing the factors that contributed to their failure. Let's take a look at what they have identified as the top ten reasons well-funded companies fail. See if you notice a recurring theme.

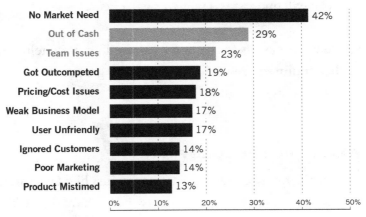

**8 OUT OF TOP 10 REASONS FOR FAILURE CAN BE AVOIDED
WITH GOOD MARKETING**

Reason	Percentage
No Market Need	42%
Out of Cash	29%
Team Issues	23%
Got Outcompeted	19%
Pricing/Cost Issues	18%
Weak Business Model	17%
User Unfriendly	17%
Ignored Customers	14%
Poor Marketing	14%
Product Mistimed	13%

Source: CB Insights, Nov 2019.

As you can see, eight of the top ten reasons for failure could have been addressed by better and timelier marketing (everything, in fact, except for "out of cash" and "team issues"). In other words, if these companies had just executed their marketing well, they might have overcome major challenges and survived. The takeaway? Underestimate the value and capabilities of the marketing function at your own peril.

At a minimum, marketing done well can improve your business performance. Often, it stands between success and utter failure.

So, why is there such a disconnect between what marketing

can do and how you currently feel about it? Keep reading, and you will understand why this gap exists.

While your reasons for feeling frustrated, underwhelmed, or disappointed are real, the value that great marketing provides is just as real.

WHERE THE LIES COME FROM

The fact is, many CEOs are data nerds, just like I was and, in many ways, still am. This convergence of hard data with customer behavior may not be obvious, which can make marketing seem almost counterintuitive. So if you're spending money like crazy on marketing and getting little or nothing in return, what is the source of the problem? Is your CMO incompetent? Dishonest? A con artist? Probably not. Actually, in most cases, there are possibly one or two contributing factors.

First, there are errors of omission.

It's entirely possible that your CMO lacks the knowledge or breadth of experience to be able to see the full "forest" and not get lost in the "trees," or worse, the "weeds." This would also hurt their ability to use your marketing dollars effectively. They may also be blind to some key pieces of the marketing puzzle and are therefore not able to deliver the big-picture impact you expect from marketing.

Second, there are errors of commission.

Eager to please, a marketer can easily overpromise and under-deliver. Over time, this causes the CEO to begin viewing the marketer, and perhaps the entire function of marketing, with suspicion. What may start as a minor misunderstanding can easily sour the relationship between marketing and the rest of the organization, making any collaboration even more difficult.

This isn't usually done with any malicious intent. Often, these may be innocent mistakes, arising from inexperience or unquestioned habits built over years of rote behavior. Whatever the case, the end result is the same: overpromising and under-delivering business results.

AN ACCIDENTAL MARKETER IS BORN

Before I go any further, let me share my own story about how I got started in marketing. Marketing was not my chosen profession. Truth be told, for the first twenty-one years of my life, I thought very poorly of "sales and marketing types." I thought they were charlatans with their hands in other people's pockets.

Indeed, my marketing career began when I was dragged into marketing.

If you're like most business leaders, you probably come from a technical or operational background. While marketing may have piqued your curiosity at some point, it has most likely primarily been a source of frustration, and perhaps outside of your comfort zone. I understand this completely. I had no intention of becoming a marketer. When I was young I loved science, math, and physics, but I really loved cars. I wanted to design cars for a living, so I planned to become a mechanical engineer. After high school, I enrolled in one of the most prestigious technical universities in the world, the Indian Institute of Technology in Delhi, India.

Unlike many of my classmates, who decided to pursue graduate degrees in engineering or management, I decided to chase my dream of joining an automotive company. I was thrilled to receive a job offer from Toyota for its first project in India. It seemed like my dream was coming true.

And then I arrived for my first day at work. The CEO of the project welcomed me and promptly informed me that I would be working in marketing!

I pleaded with him to be put on the engineering team. The CEO was sympathetic to my plight. After all, he was a mechanical engineer himself, and he confessed that he shared my low opinion of sales and marketing. Still, he insisted that my first assignment would be in marketing, because that's where the project needed my help the most. I was the nineteenth hire for the project, and only the second person on the marketing team.

Although I was less than thrilled, I accepted the position. I didn't have much leverage, and starting a career at Toyota was not something to be dismissed lightly. Plus, the CEO promised to reconsider my request to join the engineering team, in a couple of years.

To make a long story short, my first assignment involved driving across India, in a brand-new Toyota Dyna pickup prototype, and surveying the market by talking to prospective end users, dealers, and service stations. Among the many decisions we had to make, before going into production, were product features and pricing. One of the key features we had to decide on was whether or not to offer seat belts. That might seem astonishing, but remember, this was the mid80s, and there were no seat belt laws in India at the time.

Armed with what we thought was incontrovertible data, from Japan, the US, Europe, and elsewhere, that proved the value of seat belts, we traveled throughout the country, asking people how much they would pay for this lifesaving feature. To our amazement, not a single respondent said they would pay for seat belts. Not only that, but quite a few told us that they believed seat belts would make driving the vehicle less safe.

For an engineer and data nerd like me, these responses made absolutely no sense. Still, we carried on, continuing our extensive field research on a whole host of topics, by meeting and talking to our future customers and potential partners. Then one day, while driving in the remote state of Assam in eastern India, I witnessed an accident that opened our eyes. A truck had smashed its front end into a fully grown teakwood tree. Steam was pouring out of the radiator. The vehicle was obviously a wreck and a total loss, but somehow the driver and his companion (i.e., his "cleaner" in Indian trucking par-lance) were standing off to one side, miraculously unhurt.

When we inquired about the accident, we learned that the brakes on the truck had failed. Without panicking, as if following a well-practiced routine, the driver shouted for his companion to open the door and jump out right before impact. He followed his own advice concurrently, leaping to safety just before the truck slammed into the tree.

Suddenly, it all became clear.

At last, I understood why seat belts were viewed with suspi-cion across the country; the additional step of unbuckling an unfamiliar belt would cost precious seconds and make it more difficult to jump free of a vehicle, in a timely manner, during an accident. The hard, incontrovertible data was bumping up against established behavior and a mindset reinforced by years of practice.

That was the moment I discovered how the rational brain meets our own primal brain (more on this later). More significantly, I realized that good marketing must serve at the intersection of engineering/technology/data and customer behavior/mindset, some of which may well appear to be irrational. And much to my pleasant surprise, I also discovered that real marketing does not involve putting your hands in other people's pockets. Real marketing done well serves companies and their customers equally well.

An accidental marketer was born in the shadows of that teakwood tree in Assam.

While I may have been dragged into marketing, it didn't take long for me to fall in love with it. When I was given a choice to go back into engineering, as I originally intended, I decided to stay in marketing. In fact, I doubled down and formalized my education in and love for marketing, by getting an MBA from Yale University.

Throughout my career, I've had the privilege and honor of working with wonderful multinational companies in the United States and globally; I have practiced the art and science of marketing with companies including Toyota, Cummins Engine, Honeywell, and Kodak Health Imaging. Since 2012, as a partner in Chief Outsiders (a national firm providing CMOs, on a fractional basis, to emerging and midsize companies), I have been using my marketing knowledge and experience to help companies solve growth challenges.

In 2009, thanks to some good and timely advice from family and friends, I decided to take my professional marketing experience into the classroom and began teaching marketing to business students (undergraduate, graduate, and executives) at Sierra Nevada University in Lake Tahoe, and more recently at Hult International Business School's campuses in San Francisco, California, and Dubai, United Arab Emirates.

Over the years, I have taught courses in Marketing Analytics, Pricing, Introduction to Marketing, Consumer Behavior, Marketing Strategy, Business Planning, and a few more. Very quickly I discovered that teaching was not only a very good way to "give back" and prepare a new breed of marketers; it also helped me stay fresh with new marketing ideas and concepts and understand how the next generation thinks about marketing, and business in general. What a blessing to be able to teach and learn at the same time!

WHAT YOU WILL GET FROM THIS BOOK

In the following chapters, I promise to do two things for you.

First, with illustrative examples and reasoning, I will give you the insight you need to spot the "leaky holes" draining your marketing dollars. I will help you understand what marketing is—what it can do for you and, just as important, what it can't do. We will also examine some specific ways it is often misused and abused, leading to the frustrations you are likely familiar with.

Second, after you have spotted these holes, I will reveal what you can do to plug them using more effective marketing that delivers the results you have been seeking. Based on my years of research, experience, and battle scars obtained in a cross section of industries, I will provide some best practices for making marketing effective for you, your team, and your business.

In short, you will learn how to separate "lies and damned lies," from real and effective marketing.

By the time you finish this book, you will have a much better understanding of how to leverage marketing, for maximum advantage, and how to work seamlessly with your marketing team, while avoiding many common pitfalls. Armed with this knowledge, you will know if anyone tries to take you for a ride with their less-than-optimal marketing ideas. More than that, you'll have a much better understanding of the tools and techniques available for you to maximize the return on your marketing dollars and grow your business.

A NOTE TO READERS

You may have come to this book looking for help on specific marketing tactics. Indeed, you may already have deep knowledge about many aspects of marketing, but simply desire quick, practical advice about a few elements of your strategy. Rather than forcing you to wade through every chapter looking for relevant information, I have prepared a bulleted guide, which provides the basic advice being shared in each chapter. You will find this at the end of the book, after the conclusion. You are welcome to read ahead and get a quick peek at key chapter points. Of course, you can always get the details, tips, and tricks that I share (and valuable lessons from other people's mistakes) within the chapters themselves.

PART ONE

WHAT IS MARKETING?

CHAPTER ONE

LET'S DEFINE MARKETING

This is not intended to be the first book you ever read about marketing. On the contrary, my assumption is that you have read many other excellent books on the subject and have been exposed (in every sense of the word) to the practice of marketing, over the years. That said, I know from experience that it may be instructive to take some time upfront to define marketing and make sure we are on the same page.

There's a famous Indian parable that could very well be an allegory for how CEOs view and understand marketing today. Five blind men overhear that a strange new animal called an elephant has been brought into their village. They have never encountered an elephant before, so they set off to discover this animal for themselves.

Once they arrive at its pen, they reach out to feel the animal, so they can discover what sort of a creature it might be. The first man grabs its trunk and says, "Ah, I understand now. An elephant is a kind of large snake." The second man reaches out and lays his hand upon the animal's leg and says, "No, I can clearly tell that this elephant has the shape of a pillar, like a large tree."

The third man touches the side of the elephant and says, "Clearly, this elephant is flat like an enormous wall." The fourth man grabs its tail and says, "To me, this elephant is like a small rope that swings back and forth." Finally, the fifth man reaches up and feels the long tusk of the elephant and announces, confidently, "You are all wrong. I have felt this animal, and I tell you it is hard, smooth, and sharp like a spear."

In some versions of the story, the men suspect one another of lying and come to blows. In others, they begin to collaborate, pooling their knowledge to discover the true nature of the elephant. Whatever the case, it's a story that has endured. Composed sometime between 1500 and 1200 BC, it first appeared in the Rig Veda, a collection of Vedic Sanskrit hymns. However, many versions of the story have spread around the world, because there is something very human, and very true, about the story, despite its satirical nature.

What's the moral of the story?

That while truth might be singular, our perception of it varies. Also, our limited and incomplete perception of reality can cause us to draw faulty conclusions.

I thought of this story when I considered the struggles so many leaders have with marketing. Most leaders I talk to aren't wrong about marketing. Their understanding is simply limited and incomplete. They have a view of marketing based on their own narrow view of what they have personally experienced.

What we need is a big and comprehensive picture, so we can make decisions from a position of clarity and completeness. Before we dive into the specific tactics you can use to get the most out of your marketing dollar, I want to provide you with that big-picture understanding of the way marketing works. First, we'll look at the difference between sales and marketing, and then, for easier understanding, we will examine different types of marketing. This will provide a solid foundation upon which you can begin to build.

But first, an answer to the most basic question of all: what is marketing?

There are many ways to answer this question, but I believe it is most helpful to describe marketing as a bridge that connects a business with its customers and potential customers. Ideally, it's a two-way bridge: customers acquire knowledge about a company and its products while, at the same time, the company acquires knowledge about customers and the marketplace.

The two-way nature of the bridge is worth emphasizing. You need to ensure that you view marketing in a holistic manner. It's not just for communicating the value that you deliver through your products and services. It also needs to function as your conduit for learning about your customers, potential customers, competitors, and the entire marketplace in which they, and you, operate. When you improve your understanding of their relevant feelings, preferences, and experiences, you are much more likely to design and deliver better products and services that your customers will line up for.

This definition gives us an effective overview of marketing, which will prove useful as we dive into specific tactics to drive business growth.

STRIPPING AWAY THE CONFUSION

Peanut butter and jelly. Oil and vinegar. Mac and cheese. Sales and marketing. All of these are great pairings of things that also exist independently of each other. Of course, together they are even better than their individual parts.

I use the above examples to illustrate that, while every business wants (or should want) to have a cohesive sales and marketing team, many business leaders run into trouble when they confuse and conflate sales with marketing. The two are not the same; indeed, they play very different roles in your company. In clearest terms, sales is focused on the present (or the near term), while marketing is focused on the future (or the long term).

In other words, sales is about trying to get customers to purchase what is in your inventory today, while marketing is about trying to figure out what you should have in your inventory tomorrow and generating interest in that future sale. Sales is about closing a transaction fast, while marketing is about persuading your potential customers and making the job of sales easier.

In the introduction, I mentioned my fondness for automobiles. With that in mind, think of sales and marketing as headlights on your car. Sales is the low beam, providing a view of what's right in front of you. Marketing works like your high beam, providing a longer and wider view of the road ahead and the surrounding landscape. It allows you to see what's in the distance, and perhaps around the bend, and adjust accordingly. You need both beams to function well and to work well together.

When your sales team is trying to convince a customer to close a deal, that's not marketing, and it's a dangerous mistake to confuse the two. Closing deals is important, but it doesn't necessarily set you up for future success. If that's where most of your money is going, then you're not actually investing in marketing. Nor can sales take the place of marketing, because clearing out the inventory in your warehouse won't guarantee future success.

To really invest in marketing, you must aim further down the road, trying to get both a long and wide view of your potential customers and the marketplace. To do that, tactically and strategically, you need an approach that focuses on both Big-M marketing and small-m marketing.

Now, what do I mean by Big-M and small-m marketing?

MARKETING: BIG M ⟷ SMALL M

Unless you do these and get them right...	...You'll continue to <u>waste</u> at least 50% of your marketing spend.
BIG M (STRATEGIC)	**SMALL M** (TACTICAL)
Insights	**Execution**
• "Why?"	• Logos
• Company	• Promotions
• Customer	• Lead generation
• Competition	• Websites
Strategy	• Sales collateral
• Segmentation	• Testimonials
• Product/Service design	• Social media
• Differentiation	• Event marketing
• Positioning	• Advertising
• Pricing	• Public relations
• Messaging	• Metrics

Big-M marketing refers to foundational aspects of marketing that help define your business strategy. It sets the stage and reveals a path (or multiple paths) that will get you the business results you desire. Big-M marketing is about gaining rich insights, from your customers, and a strong understanding of your competitive landscape. Equally important, it's about gaining a deep, introspective understanding of your own company, its team and capabilities, and the limitations that can make all the difference between a strategy that collects dust on a bookshelf and one that delivers results.

Small-m marketing refers to the tactics you can implement

to move the needle. It also happens to be the more visible part of marketing: your website, logo, brochures, tagline, color scheme, content generation, SEO, advertisements, and so on.

We can further subdivide small-m marketing into two categories:

- Activities that make an immediate, short-term impact. If you change your company logo, for example, customers are either going to like or dislike it. Either way, they will have an immediate reaction. Six months down the road, however, it probably won't make much of a difference to your company's financial wellbeing. Your new logo will become the norm, and life will go on.
- Activities that take time to make an impact. Some of your small-m tactics might take a while to gain traction and get a noticeable response from customers. However, if done well, these tactics' impact could be long-lasting. This includes tactics like Search Engine Optimization (SEO), advertising, publishing blog articles, and so forth. While you might not see instant results from any of these tactics, if you do them well, they will begin to influence customers and potential customers, over time, in a longer-lasting manner.

TWO COMPONENTS OF SMALL M

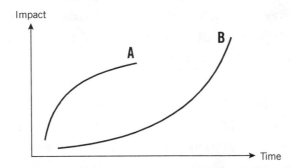

A	Short-term; diminishing returns

Branding & logotype

Pay for lists

Focus on homepage

Cold calling

Focus on press releases

Throw parties and events

Make more noise through followers

Outsource core marketing

PPC & Adwords

Link building

B	Long-term; scalable

A/B testing

Build opt-in lists

Focus on landing pages

Great customer service

Get subscribers to your blog

Create educational content

Participate in long tail social media

Invest in being relevant

Earn clicks with great content

Develop trusted relationships

It's important for leaders to understand these two sub-categories of small-m marketing, so they have realistic expectations about the timing of the outcomes of their various marketing initiatives.

For instance, if you change the color scheme of your website and get some instant positive feedback, you shouldn't assume this will translate into an ever-increasing boost in sales that will last for many months or years.

On the other hand, just because you hire someone to manage your SEO, for $5,000 a month, doesn't mean you're going to see substantial results by the second month. Indeed, it might take almost a full year before the results of that investment can be realized.

Understand the timeframe of your tactics, and you will have realistic expectations for the outcome. This will also help you prioritize and match your investments with realistic revenue goals.

As you can imagine, most of your time and dollars are going to be spent on small-m marketing, and that's how it should be. Indeed, it will also remain the more visible part of any marketing effort. However, most leakage of marketing dollars happens in small-m marketing tactics, largely because most businesses jump straight into small-m stuff without investing the necessary time and effort in building a foundation that comes only with Big-M marketing.

Just as a strong foundation is essential for a sturdy, long-lasting house, the time spent on Big-M marketing is critical to ensure that your small-m tactics continue to be as effective as they can be. To paraphrase an old Fram oil filter commercial, "Spend a little more on Big-M marketing now, or spend a lot-more-than-necessary on small-m marketing the rest of your life."

PUT THE ULTIMATE CUSTOMER AT THE CENTER

In all of this, it's important to remember that great marketing always places the ultimate customer at the center of everything, regardless of whether you're working with Big-M or small-m, short term or long term. The ultimate customer refers to the person or group who will end up using your product or service. In the end, you must come to understand this person and focus all of your efforts in their direction. This is true even if you never sell directly to your end user.

Know the marketplace where they operate. Get a clear picture of the landscape around them. Understand how they live, how they think, how they feel, and what things affect them. To get the most impact from your marketing dollars, your foundation, and the tactics you construct on top of that foundation must all be directed toward that ultimate customer—not the distributor or dealer.

Consider this. Toyota is the largest manufacturer of cars and trucks in the world, in terms of revenue. Their customers live in over 170 countries around the world. However, they don't actually sell directly to customers. Instead, they sell their vehicles to distributors, and those distributors have local dealers who sell them to individuals like you and me. Nevertheless, Toyota spends almost its entire marketing budget on its end customers, with only a small portion going toward its distributors or dealers—the actual businesses that buy from Toyota to sell to people like you and me.

By focusing all of its marketing on the individuals who buy and use their cars and trucks (their ultimate customers), Toyota impacts the entire value and supply chain, including distributors and dealers.

Likewise, for the most part, Samsung doesn't sell televisions directly to customers. They sell them to retailers like Best Buy or Costco. However, when it comes to their marketing efforts, they focus on shoppers who will come into retail stores and buy their products. Best Buy, Costco, Walmart, and other stores are simply intermediaries between Samsung and their ultimate customers, and they all benefit from Samsung's marketing targeted at their end users.

For maximum impact, focus on your ultimate customer in everything you do, even if you never directly interact with them. When you do that, you will also be effectively marketing to your intermediaries. Good channel partners will always appreciate and reward you for anything you do to make their selling job easier.

RIDING THE ELEPHANT

Remember: an elephant is more than just a trunk, or a leg, or a belly, or a tail, or a tusk. You must understand how all of these parts fit together to create the whole animal. Only then will you understand how you can climb on its back and guide it to where you want to go.

Similarly, once you understand how each of the different pieces of marketing fit together—both Big-M and small-m— you can bring them together, in an effective way, to grow your business, now and into the future.

PART TWO

BIG-M MARKETING

—

CHAPTER TWO

LEFT BRAIN OR RIGHT BRAIN

In 1997, Steve Jobs delivered what would become a landmark speech on Apple's approach to marketing. He had returned as CEO, twelve years after being forced to resign, and now faced the difficult task of rebuilding the company from the ground up. Here is what he said in that speech:

> This is a very noisy world, and we're not going to get a chance to get people to remember much about us. No company is. And so, we have to be really clear on what we want them to know about us...The way to do that is not to talk about speeds and feeds. It's not to talk about bits and megahertz. It's not to talk about why we're better than Windows...Our customers want to know who is Apple and what is it that we stand for? Where do we fit in this world? And what we are about isn't making boxes for people to get their jobs done, although we do that well. We do that, better than almost anybody in some

cases. But Apple's about something more than that. Apple at the core—its core value is that we believe that people with passion can change the world for the better.[1]

At the time, the marketing focus of most computer companies was all about the superiority of their technology. Companies like Dell, Compaq, IBM, and Lenovo appealed to the left brain, the logic center, by championing their hardware specs: "We offer sixteen megabytes of RAM and 800 megabytes of storage at a reasonable price!"

But Steve Jobs realized that the technical specs, which he called "speeds and feeds," don't matter all that much in marketing. At least, one should not lead with them. Instead of simply boasting about the technology, Apple needed to tug at people's emotions by providing an inspiring vision and values that would resonate with potential customers. That became the focus of Apple's marketing. It was perhaps the most visible and impactful recognition of the role the right brain plays in decision making, and we've all seen the results: Apple has created a vast and loyal fan base, which believes in both the company and their products.

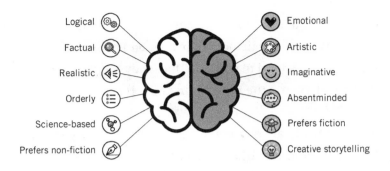

Logical
Factual
Realistic
Orderly
Science-based
Prefers non-fiction

Emotional
Artistic
Imaginative
Absentminded
Prefers fiction
Creative storytelling

HANDLING NIGERIAN PRINCES

Let's consider another example that I am sure we all experience every day.

On a typical weekday, I receive a little more than 400 emails. These emails run the gamut from ads for tech products to heartfelt messages from long-lost Nigerian princes who apparently need my help (and bank account and social security numbers) to get their fortunes back.

Out of these 400 emails, I typically only read about twenty-five to thirty of them, either because I need the information or I recognize the sender, or because the sender somehow grabs my attention. Of those twenty-five to thirty, I usually reply to somewhere between five and ten of them. Think about that. Out of the 400 emails I receive daily, only five to ten lead me to take an action other than simply hitting delete.

Marketers have a very limited amount of time to convince me to give their email more than a second or two of my time, much less respond to it. To do that, they are going to have to appeal to both the right brain and left brain.

In this age of data overload, it's not easy for lowly email to stand out and be noticed. One of the ways these market-ers could improve the odds of getting noticed—and maybe even getting me to respond—is to first appeal to my right (creative/artistic) brain, by convincing me that it's worth my time to let my left (data hungry) brain sift through the data they've provided to make their case. Just giving me more (and more) dry data is not going to grab my attention.

WHAT YOU CAN'T MEASURE

Think about all of those poor souls, sending out emails day after day, week after week, with their fingers crossed, hoping that maybe—just maybe—this time I will notice and open it. Of course, most of them are tracking various met-rics related to their emails, tweaking things in an attempt to boost those open rates. As the old saying goes, "What doesn't get measured doesn't get improved."

The problem is, some of the most important elements of customer engagement can't be measured. Yes, you can track your open rate, click rate, and a lot of other interac-tions, but how do you measure the emotional response of the people you're trying to reach? How do you measure whether or not you're tugging at their heartstrings?

Good marketing isn't just about finding more people to reach or how efficiently you're reaching them. It's also about how strongly you're impacting your audience, on an emotional level, and that's not a data point you can readily track.

Thus the real power of marketing comes from synergy of both the left brain (data) and the right brain (emotion). I want to give you a simple process for doing just that.

- Step One: make an emotional appeal. In all of your marketing efforts, start by first relating with your audience and their likely pain points and desires.
- Step Two: provide a short, simple list of benefits of your product or service. It might be tempting to overload your audience, with every bit of data you have, but you will be better served by being selective. Get to know your target audience, and give them just the high points of how your product or service will solve their pain points or serve their desires.
- Step Three: prove it. Once your audience is attracted to the benefits you've claimed, they will certainly be looking for proof points. This could take the form of testimonials, demos, datasheets, or facts and figures. The more personal you can make these, the better the response you are likely to get.

- Step Four: track & measure. It will be useful for you to track and measure key metrics of how your target audience is responding. Keep in mind, however, that some of the most important things—like the emotional connection your message is making—can't be measured easily.

In these four steps, you can see a combination of left brain and right brain activities, using both hard data and emotional appeals to make the greatest impact on your audience.

If you apply these four steps, as you think about your marketing initiatives, you will address both the left and right brains of your audience. Put another way, the road to great marketing is paved with data. But this data must be delivered to your decision makers in a gift wrap that evokes a positive emotional response, making them want to process the necessary data to make a favorable decision.

I've placed this advice at the beginning of our section on Big-M marketing, because it will help provide you with the right mindset moving forward. As we proceed through the next chapters, I recommend applying this mindset to everything we discuss.

CHAPTER THREE

BEING RATIONAL ABOUT IRRATIONALITY

According to Dr. Sigmund Freud, "Humanity is in the highest degree irrational, so that there is no prospect of influencing it by reasonable arguments." While he said this in the context of therapy, I believe it could just as easily apply to buyers and sellers.

There's a little experiment I like to run when I'm teaching a marketing class. Try it the next time you're in a group setting. First, I produce a twenty-dollar bill. Then I announce, "I am going to auction this twenty-dollar bill right now. Bids will start at one dollar and increase in one-dollar increments. The highest bidder will receive the twenty-dollar bill. But here's the catch: the second highest bidder also has to pay me their bid and get nothing in return."

It doesn't take long to get the bidding process going. After all, getting twenty dollars for one dollar is a pretty good deal—a fact that is not lost on anyone! Then someone else bids two dollars. Then someone bids three. At this point, bidders are still very excited at the prospect of getting in on this obvious bargain.

If it stops at this point, the highest bidder gets a pretty good deal, the second-highest bidder isn't out much money, and I receive both of their bids, which means I am only out fifteen bucks.

However, it never stops there.

Indeed, unless there's some collusion, the bidding generally continues: five bucks, six, seven, eight. Inevitably, someone will eventually bid twenty dollars, even though this means they will break even. I lose the original twenty-dollar bill, but I gain both of the high bids, making a profit of nineteen bucks. It's a good deal for me, a neutral deal for the highest bidder, and a very bad deal for the second-highest bidder.

Believe it or not, it rarely ends here.

As the spirit of competition (and loss minimization) takes hold, the bids continue. Someone bids twenty-one dollars. More often than not, this bid comes from the same person who previously bid nineteen (and lost), as they think it is better to lose only a dollar (the last bid of twenty-one dollars minus the value of twenty) rather than losing nineteen dollars (the previous bid, with nothing to show for it).

It still doesn't stop there. The person who was sheepishly willing to take the break-even deal of paying twenty bucks for a twenty-dollar bill now faces a loss of twenty bucks. By bidding twenty-two dollars, this person hopes to reduce their loss from twenty dollars to two, provided the game ends at this point.

Again, it rarely ends here. Why? The reason is simple. No one wants to be the second-highest bidder, because they're going to lose everything. It's better to pay twenty-five and get back twenty than to pay twenty-four and get nothing. This loss-minimization routine is likely to continue, until the increasing level of frustration forces one of the bidders to stop the process and chalk up their loss to a life lesson, which they are keen to monetize on other willing and gullible participants in the future!

Let's look at another experiment, conducted at Harvard in 1995. A professor gave students two choices: one, you can make $50,000 a year while living in a neighborhood where everyone around you makes $25,000; or two, you can make $100,000 a year while living in a neighborhood where everyone around you makes $200,000.

Assuming the cost of living is the same in both instances, the choice should be clear, shouldn't it? With the second one, you receive twice the income. However, the professor found that roughly half the class preferred the first option. When he asked why, students expressed their inherent desire to "do better than the Joneses." They put significant, implicit value on living around people who made significantly less money than them.

TEST YOUR RATIONAL SELF

While these examples of human behavior might seem somewhat contrived and borderline ridiculous, don't assume that you are above this. You are human, too, and likely prone to irrational decisions as well.

Here's a test for you.

I'm going to flip a coin, and you can win some money depending on how it lands. Choose one of these two options:

GAME 1	
Option 1 ☐	**Option 2** ☐
Win $5,000 for sure	***Heads:*** *Win $10,000* ***Tails:*** *Win $0*

- Option A: whether it lands on heads or tails, you win $5,000.
- Option B: if it lands on heads, you get $10,000. If it lands on tails, you get nothing.

Which option would you choose? State your choice before reading on.

With the first, you are guaranteed to win $5,000, but with the second you get either $10,000 or nothing. Most people go with Option A because it's a sure thing.

Now, let's play this game again, but change the outcomes a little. Which of these would you choose?

GAME 2

Option 1 ☐	Option 2 ☐
Lose $5,000	**Heads:** *Lose $10,000*
for sure	**Tails:** *Lose $0*

- Option A: whether the coin lands on heads or tails, you lose $5,000.
- Option B: if it lands on heads, you lose $10,000, but if it lands on tails, you lose nothing.

Which one would you choose now?

Most people will choose Option B this time. They are willing to take a chance and potentially lose $10,000, just to avoid the "sure thing" loss of $5,000 that comes with the first option.

Mathematically, the expected value of each pair of options in each situation is the same—an expected gain of $5,000 in the first case, an expected loss of $5,000 in the second case. However, our responses to these two situations are very different, reflecting our inherent "loss aversion" bias. Loss aversion bias is one of 188 distinct cognitive biases recognized by science. Simply put, it indicates that most of us are more sensitive, and keener to avoid a loss than to get a win or pleasure.

Clearly, a complex array of emotions, motivations, perceptions, and preferences influence us in unexpected ways. Human beings don't always make the simplest, most mathematically astute, or rational choices.

WHEN FACTS ALONE DON'T WORK

You've probably already witnessed the human tendency toward irrational decision-making in your own business. Have you ever presented all of the facts to a prospective customer, proving, with hard data, that your product or service is the best for meeting their needs, only to have the customer end up choosing someone else's product or service?

It's frustrating, and you might wonder, "How can a rational person choose the competitor when they know that we offer a better product in every way?"

The answer, of course, is that people aren't always rational.

Let's be clear; irrational behavior is not the same as random behavior. In his book Predictably Irrational, Dan Ariely, a professor of psychology and behavioral economics at Duke University, makes a strong case that human irrationality is highly predictable.

We are patchwork beings comprised of many cognitive biases. In fact, there is one specific cognitive bias that you will encounter a lot in your sales and marketing efforts. It's called immediacy bias. It's our tendency to prefer an instant reward to a more valuable, long-term reward.

Put another way, it means people are hardwired to put greater value on the here and now. If they can get a small reward now, even at the cost of some greater reward years in the future, they will be strongly tempted to take the small reward. It's the reason why shoppers will drive twenty extra miles, to a grocery store in the next town, just because milk is on sale there now, ignoring the cost of extra gas they will need to replace later.

What does immediacy bias look like in marketing? Let's suppose your product is better than your competitor's in every way, and will deliver far more value to the user over its lifetime; however, your competitor's product is cheaper.

From your customer's point of view, this price saving is immediate and now, whereas the benefits, even when presented in a compelling and believable manner, are going to be realized over a much longer period of time. Even if you show the customer hard data that proves your product will save them a lot more in the long run, the here-and-now savings from a lower price will still be a huge factor in their decision.

As an aside, this is the reason why so many people in the United States find themselves with less than adequate savings for retirement.

A smart marketer will be aware of this and communicate with customers accordingly. Hard data about long-term benefits must be balanced with some inclusion of immediate and short-term benefits as well.

Companies like TJ Maxx and Marshall's understand this well and market their products accordingly. These stores' price tags feature their instore price placed beside a much higher compare-at price. They never say where the higher price comes from, but customers see the difference and get that small endorphin hit: "Wow, I'm saving so much today!"

Another way to deal with this immediacy bias is to lean on the findings of Nobel laureate Daniel Kahneman, one of only three people to win the Nobel in economics who were not trained in classical economics. In his book Thinking, Fast and Slow, Kahneman explains that people need to gain 1.5–2.5 times more than what they stand to lose before they will agree to the transaction.

In other words, if you want to sell something for ten dollars, the buyer must be convinced that they're going to get fifteen to twenty-five dollars' worth of value out of their purchase. This ratio alone puts additional pressure on you to make sure you and your team are effectively marketing to your prospects.

UNDERSTANDING PEOPLE

At the end of the day, a big part of a marketer's job is to understand how people think, feel, and make decisions. They must learn to recognize and understand the irrationality and cognitive biases that we all have and use this knowledge to predict and influence customer behavior. Great marketers recognize how our rational and primal brains work simultaneously, but often at cross purposes, to influence our decisions. They use this knowledge to create marketing programs that blend the use of data with emotional cues, and feed both our primal and rational brains for the desired effect.

Antonio Damasio, a neuroscientist and professor at the University of Southern California, has famously said, "We are not thinking machines that feel, we are feeling machines that often think." Emotions are a deciding factor, in a majority of our decisions, so instead of thinking and acting, we often feel and act. Keep this in mind with your messaging, and you will begin to appeal to potential customers far more effectively.

CHAPTER FOUR

RICHES ARE IN NICHES... BUT NOT IN TRENCHES

Let me be straight with you: specialization is a good thing. I'm a big believer in specialization. Indeed, if you get anything meaningful out of an MBA, it's learning the value of segmentation and picking your targets. Many CEOs have learned the value of specialization, whether through their education or experience, and it's a good thing. That's why the first part of this chapter title is "Riches are in Niches."

But that is not the whole story.

Let me give you a more complete, albeit nuanced, viewpoint. For most companies, defining their specialization in terms of industry verticals is a mistake. Counterintuitively, this is especially true when a company is just starting out.

Wait a minute. Did I just say it's good to specialize and then say it's a huge mistake to specialize? Am I speaking out of both sides of my mouth? No, but you can set yourself up for some real trouble down the road if you specialize too early or if you define your specialization in terms of your customers' verticals.

Let's suppose you're a small business just getting started. You win your first big contract in a specific vertical. For the sake of this example, let's say your first major customer is a healthcare company. You go to work, fulfill the contract, and do a great job. After you've spent some time servicing that client, you feel like you're now an expert in the healthcare industry.

While it's true that you now know more about healthcare than other businesses, your real points of differentiation are not likely to include your healthcare knowledge based solely upon this one client. Your next healthcare client is unlikely to give you their business just because your first and only client thus far was in the same industry. It's better to look for other points of differentiation.

If you are struggling to find these points of differentiation for your business, it may be very illuminating for you to seek some candid feedback and have some deep conversations with your early clients. Ask them what they saw in you that made them give you their business. Did they see any other positive (or negative) points of differentiation during the course of their dealings with you? All of this will help you refine your own messaging and positioning for future clients and customers.

Let me illustrate this with a true story.

Not long ago, I was invited to dinner by the CEO of a small software company in Austin, Texas. He was looking for some fresh ideas about how he could grow his business. The company was only a year old, but he'd already done great work for a real estate company and a healthcare company. In fact, those first two experiences had gone so well that he was now thinking about specializing in healthcare and real estate verticals.

"I think I found our niches," he said. "We will focus our business development on these two verticals. What do you think?"

"Don't do it," I replied.

He seemed taken aback by my response. After staring at me in confusion for a second, he said, "Well, we have to specialize in something, don't we? My company can't be everything to everybody. Surely we've found our niches."

"What is your company good at?" I asked. "What is your

unique selling proposition that gives you an edge? Yes, you had two great clients, each in a specific industry, but what did you do for them that made them happy?"

As we talked, I discovered that there were two things in particular that these initial clients had appreciated and benefited from: First, an excellent user experience (UX) provided by an attractive and convenient user interface (UI). Second, unlike most software companies that have their operations in India, the Philippines, or Ukraine, this Texas company had all of its operations in Guadalajara, Mexico. The geographic and time-zone proximity offered a clear and obvious advantage to its target audience of US-based companies, since it enabled them to communicate with clients in real time, during business hours, and make face-to-face visits more affordable and possible.

I wrote these down for him: "UX/UI and geographic proximity."

"These are your points of differentiation and should be part of your marketing focus," I said. "Instead of limiting yourself to two specific industries, right out of the gate, thereby reducing the number of opportunities, focus on these two things in your marketing. Instead of saying, 'We're healthcare and real estate experts,' position yourselves as experts in UX/UI. Remind your potential targets of the inconvenience, pains, and hidden costs associated with working across multiple time zones and long distances."

I could tell this was a revelation to the CEO. From that point forward, he began to think about marketing his company in a whole new way. Rather than narrowing his focus and reducing the number of potential clients dramatically, he was able to discover a few unique and relevant points of differentiation. This enabled him to position his business, much more uniquely and effectively, to create greater and more diverse opportunities for growth.

FOCUS ON WHAT YOU DO BEST

Focus is great, and the old saying is true: riches are indeed found in niches. However, too many businesses use verticals as their focus and, in so doing, limit their future growth unnecessarily by leaving their own real points of differentiation muddled up and hidden.

If you specialize too narrowly—and, by that, I mean in one or two verticals—you may soon discover the problems that come with putting all of your eggs in one or two baskets. All businesses experience some level of cyclicality. Having a diverse portfolio of clients from different industries and verticals is a good way to reduce your own business cyclicality.

Discover your own unique traits and expertise, and present them to any and all who might appreciate what you bring to the table. This will put you in a much stronger position for long-term, sustained growth.

CHAPTER FIVE

IT'S ALL DIGITAL NOW

It was a class of new marketing students, and I was teaching them about various marketing channels in both digital and traditional media. As we approached the halfway point, a young, bright-eyed student in the front row raised his hand.

"Sir, why don't we cut to the chase and just focus on digital marketing?" he asked. "After all, it's all digital now."

I've encountered this line of thinking numerous times, in recent years, not only from students but also from business executives.

Everything has gone digital, right? So, shouldn't we focus all of our efforts on digital marketing?

"If that's the case," I replied, "then thirty years ago, when

I was a marketing student, my professor would have spent at least some of our class time teaching us all about the printing press."

Of course, my professor didn't spend a single solitary moment talking about the technical details of the printing press. Why? Because the printing press is simply an enabler—one of many available to marketers, then and now.

How can you tell when it's more effective to use traditional marketing rather than digital marketing? To do that, you need to take into account the entire customer journey, represented here as an infinity loop.

BUYER'S JOURNEY—CUSTOMER LOOP

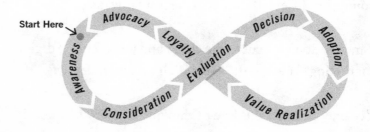

Touching, Nurturing, and Serving Prospects and Customers at Each Step

At each step of the customer journey, consider how your target audience is consuming information. What channels are they using, and what medium will be the most accessible to them?

Let me give you a few more illustrative examples of how traditional channels have been used creatively—and sometimes in concert with—digital channels for very effective and impactful campaigns.

FOLLOWING THE CUSTOMER'S JOURNEY

Starbucks has a strong digital marketing presence, but they also try to capture people when they're waiting at the bus stop or train station, driving to work, or walking to the office downtown. To do that, they invest in both online ads and billboards, posters, and print ads. Starbucks' goal is to get the attention of customers and potential customers at every step of their journey. They want that young professional woman sitting at the train station to look up, see a colorful Starbucks poster on the wall, and think, "I could really use a grande café latte right now." At that moment, a digital ad on her Facebook page might not have the same impact.

In 2018, Nestlé ran a brilliant promotion for their Kit Kat Chunky candy bar, using traditional media. They sent postcard ads that resembled parcel delivery notices through traditional mail. The ads were personalized and contained the receiver's name and address, along with the message, "Sorry, we couldn't deliver. It's too CHUNKY for your mailbox." The copy then went on to encourage the recipient to take the notice to the nearest grocery store and collect their Kit Kat Chunky.

We tend to think of junk mail as a very old-fashioned marketing technique, but it made Kit Kat's Chunky campaign stand out. Could they have put a digital coupon on Facebook, Twitter, and Instagram instead? Certainly...and relatively few people would have noticed or paid attention. It would have simply disappeared into the flood of digital ads promising discounts and free samples.

When Apple launched AirPods Pro in major cities around the globe, they took a similar approach, using another "outdated" advertising method, to great effect. In this case, it was a series of billboards, placed strategically in places like Dubai, London, and Milan, that contained pictures of happy people dancing and listening to music. The words Apple and AirPods were nowhere to be seen, nor was the product visible on any of the billboards.

The billboards were up for three or four weeks with no explanation, giving people plenty of time to look at them and wonder what they were all about. Curiosity grew, people began to talk and speculate, and when Apple finally launched the product, all they had to do was add a bit of additional information to the billboards.

The advantage of this billboard campaign was that it allowed Apple to create suspense in a highly visible way. Because these were billboards rather than online ads, it became more of a public event. Friends and family would comment on the ads, as they passed by, so when Apple finally revealed the product, they were already part of the public conversation. Even though we usually use the phrase "viral marketing" in the digital arena, these Apple billboards created a buzz that went "viral." It was traditional advertising, albeit with a twist, at its best!

DIGITAL IS SIMPLY A MEDIUM

As my marketing professor understood, digital is simply a form of medium or channel, one of many, that can be used for marketing. Digital tools are very different from the printing press, and the time it takes to "go to print" in digital is much shorter. However, the core principles of marketing, including customer psychology, remain the same. That's why you can't simply focus on digital. Marketing needs to be viewed much more holistically.

Indeed, if you focus exclusively on digital tools, you're likely to get bogged down in the black hole of marketing, with no understanding of why you aren't achieving your desired results. The market is absolutely saturated with digital tools, options, and platforms, and they've created so much noise that potential customers just tune most of them out.

More than ever, you have to find creative ways to stand out and get your message heard. By relying on the core principles of marketing, you will not only be able to identify the right channel mix to use (digital and/or traditional), but you will also know how to refine the message you convey through these various channels.

In a world drowning in digital ads, a billboard, print ad, or poster can have a surprising impact. By doing things a little differently, you will set yourself apart. If you only focus on digital, under the mistaken belief that it's all digital now, you might miss out on some excellent marketing opportunities that traditional media offers, especially considering the fact that there's a lot less noise in the traditional ad space these days.

Traditional media still plays a significant role in our lives. Most people still watch TV, from time to time, and many listen to the radio, especially when commuting. Therefore, it's in your best interest to find your own optimal and healthy balance between digital and traditional channels of marketing.

MEDIUMS CHANGE, HUMAN BEHAVIOR DOES NOT

Mediums rise and fall in popularity (and perhaps rise again) over time, but human behavior remains roughly the same. The human brain continues to receive messages and stimuli in a similar manner, even as the pace of digital evolution continues to increase.

When it comes to marketing, you can't afford to rule out any medium if it will help you reach your target audience and catch their attention. If you pour everything into digital alone, you might miss out on some golden opportunities to stand out from the crowd. Consider the customer journey carefully. Identify the best ways to reach your audience at every step, using any medium that will do the job effectively.

Don't view traditional marketing as archaic and old-fashioned. Both digital and traditional belong within the field of marketing. Think of digital marketing as yet another method you can use, along with all of the others, to make a bigger impact on customers. Yes, digital marketing is an incredibly important method, but it's certainly not the only one.

CHAPTER SIX

YES, OUR CFO
MANAGES PRICING

A study conducted a few years ago analyzed the impact of five operating levers on the bottom line of any business:

1. price
2. revenue
3. cost of goods sold
4. selling, general, and administrative expenses
5. research and development

Specifically, researchers were trying to understand how each of these independently impacts the overall profitability of an organization. The study concluded that a change in pricing makes the biggest impact on the bottom line, as you can see in this chart.[2]

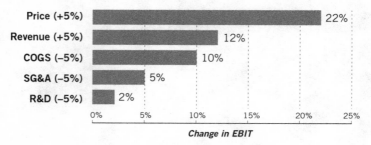

IMPACT OF OPERATING LEVERS ON PROFIT

Price (+5%)	22%
Revenue (+5%)	12%
COGS (−5%)	10%
SG&A (−5%)	5%
R&D (−5%)	2%

0% — 5% — 10% — 15% — 20% — 25%

Change in EBIT

Source: Hinterhuber, Andreas. "Toward value-based pricing—An integrative framework for decision making", *Industrial Marketing Management, 2004.*

Clearly then, the price of your product matters and has a more significant impact on the health and wellbeing of your company—for good or ill—than just about anything else. Setting or changing prices demands careful consideration and should not be done lightly.

But who should be making these decisions?

The truth is that, in most organizations, pricing decisions are made by the chief financial officer (CFO). Very few companies have a dedicated pricing function or person managing pricing. In my own research, I've found that less than 10 percent of business schools offer a course dedicated to pricing. Typically, the subject is folded into one or two other marketing classes as a single chapter.

What is the impact of this? Simply put, most businesses

are missing out on the most significant lever in improving their profitability.

WHO SHOULD SET THE PRICE?

Who should set and manage prices? As the saying goes, where you stand on an issue often depends on where you sit.

If the CEO designates the sales leader to be in charge of pricing, because they are "the closest to the customer," a certain bias in pricing decisions will result. Sales is responsible for—and is often incentivized by—the basis of revenue generated (and not on profit). This is despite the fact that profitability is (or should be) the lifeblood of any business. Thus, with sales in charge of pricing, there's an inherent bias to lower prices so sales revenue (and commissions) can be increased.

If the CFO is responsible for setting and managing prices, you get a different set of biases. Typically, CFOs have a good handle on the cost structure of products and services. They also have a close understanding of the CEO's expectations about profit. Thus, they feel empowered to take this understanding of unit costs, add expected profit on top of it, and set the price from there.

That said, CFOs also lack an understanding of how prices might impact sales volume and customers' perception of value in products and services being provided. The math they use might work for a single unit (cost + desired profit markup = customer price), but there's no analysis of what a specific price will do to market demand. Remember, the psychology of the target audience is also at play. Failing to take this into consideration can lead to some real market blunders, even if the unit math makes sense upfront.

THE PSYCHOLOGY OF PRICING

Netflix provided us with the perfect cautionary tale to illustrate this point, back in 2011, when they made a significant pricing decision without taking into consideration how it might impact customer behavior and response. You might remember when the company announced that they were going to bifurcate their streaming and DVD rental services. Rather than receiving both services for a single price, customers would now be charged separately. The streaming service would continue to be called Netflix, while the now-separate DVD rental service would be called Qwikster, and each would have its own webpage.

No doubt the math made sense. Some executives may have even presented this dual strategy as being customer-centric. After all, they were offering both services, and customers were at liberty to choose either or both, depending on their preference.

Customers responded with almost universal derision, seeing this move as Netflix gouging them twice for the same utility of movie watching. They also hated the prospect of having to navigate two separate webpages. Over the course of four months, Netflix lost over 75 percent of its total value, along with hundreds of thousands of subscribers. The company ultimately scrapped the Qwikster concept.[3]

Interestingly, and to their credit, Netflix went on to make significant pricing changes in subsequent years and handled each of them well. A single, disastrous decision was followed by a number of successful decisions. The key difference was the way Netflix incorporated a deep understanding of their customers and their psychology, which was reflected in how they communicated these changes in the marketplace.

At an earnings call, when Netflix CEO, Reed Hastings, was asked if the company planned to make any further price changes, he responded, "I think it's a tricky thing because it really has to be a reflection of the underlying quality of the experience on a relative basis. So, as long as we're able to continue to improve our content and our whole experience at a remarkable rate...then asking our customers to help us fund that at higher levels is reasonable. But if we weren't gaining relative value for the customers, then we wouldn't be changing prices."[4]

Reed Hastings's quote is important—he clearly understands the strong relationship between pricing, customer value, and customer satisfaction.

CEOs, of course, have the ultimate authority and responsibility for managing all of these elements. However, the best people within an organization to understand both sides—profit margins and market demand—are marketers. Thus, pricing should be their responsibility to manage.

My suggestion does not come out of left field. If you recall your business training, you no doubt remember the four Ps of marketing: product, price, place, and promotion. Since price is a key aspect of marketing, it makes sense to let marketing handle it, because they will also view pricing in the context of the other three Ps.

While I have you thinking about pricing, let me offer a few more considerations.

Quite frankly, sometimes a problem that looks like a pricing issue is actually a problem with positioning and messaging. A sales leader might look at customer responses to prices and conclude that customers believe their product is too expensive, so prices should be slashed. A good marketer, on the other hand, might look at the same situation and realize that positioning and messaging need to be adjusted to communicate the value of the product more effectively.

Often, a higher price might bring you more sales, as customers perceive a higher price to be indicative of greater value. Honestly, how many times have you selected wine based on the price?

You don't have to answer that question. Instead, let me share a personal story.

Several years ago, I hosted a Thanksgiving dinner with some close friends and their daughter. As we chatted, the wife mentioned that her Sony laptop was on the fritz, and she was looking for a replacement. She asked for my recommendation, and I told her I only buy MacBooks and can thus only recommend a MacBook model.

"Oh, MacBooks are too expensive," she replied. "I'm not spending that much on a laptop."

The following day—which was, conveniently, Black Friday—her laptop finally died. Over breakfast, she told me that she planned to buy a replacement later that day.

"How much did you pay for your Sony?" I asked.

"Nine hundred dollars," she replied.

"When did you buy it?"

"Three years ago."

"And what is that Sony laptop worth now?"

She shook her head. "Nothing," she replied. "It's worthless."

"A new MacBook will cost you about $1,200," I said. "I'll make a deal with you. If you pay me $900, the original cost of your Sony laptop, I will pay the difference for a brand-new MacBook Air with similar specs to the Sony laptop you're replacing. You use it for three years—the lifespan of your Sony—then give it back to me, and we'll consider it a closed deal. How does that sound?"

"Why would you make this deal?" she asked.

"Because I know, from experience, that I will be able to resell that MacBook in three years for about $500," I said. "That means I'll get more than what I will pay from my own pocket for you to get this MacBook Air for the price of a Sony laptop."

It was a sincere offer, and my friend perceived it as such. The messaging made an impact. In the end, she decided to pay for the MacBook Air herself, and she is still using it to this day, more than seven years later.

What's the point of this story? My friend's perception of the value of MacBook Air changed when she connected the higher price with higher value. As you may have noticed, I refocused my friend's mind from price to value. Once this shift was made, the higher price of MacBook Air was not only not a hindrance anymore, but it was now reflective of implicit higher value. Exactly what Apple would have wanted to achieve!

Similarly, the Apple iPhone is not the lowest priced smartphone on the market, by any means. But somehow, they continue to sell very well. Customers perceive a long-term value that makes the purchase and ownership of an iPhone attractive and worthwhile, even at a higher price. That is the key!

You have to go beyond the math, beyond the profit margin, to look at the psychology of pricing. This is where your marketing team is best suited to make decisions. For that reason, I strongly encourage you to put pricing in the hands of your CMO.

CHAPTER SEVEN

SPEED (ALONE) KILLS

According to the Roman historian Suetonius, Emperor Augustus had a favorite saying: "Festina lente." It means, "Make haste slowly." The emperor loved this saying so much that he adopted it as his own personal motto. He even minted coins that contained an image of a hare with a snail's shell.

Augustus despised making hasty military decisions, preferring a measured approach that was more assured of success. As he often said, "That which has been done well has been done quickly enough."[5]

I came across the phrase "festina lente" some years ago, and it got me thinking. At first, I wasn't sure what to make of this apparent oxymoron. However, as I contemplated its strategic meaning, I realized the power behind it. "Make haste slowly" means proceeding deliberately, with due diligence and attention to essential detail, rather than moving as quickly as possible. Note the emphasis of the word essential; this is not a recommendation for paralysis by analysis.

As I considered the implications of "festina lente," I wondered how it might apply to marketing.

THE TORTOISE AND THE HARE, VERSION 2.0

If you're like most CEOs, you probably have a Type A personality, typified by ambition and impatience. You like to move fast, and you want things done yesterday. The business world is full of leaders rushing as fast as they can to meet deadlines, hit milestones, and beat the competition to the punch.

The problem is that speed can be deceptively lethal. It's a lot worse to move fast, in the wrong direction, than it is to move slowly in the right direction. This can be illustrated with a modified version of Aesop's classic fable, "The Tortoise and the Hare." In the original story, the hare loses the race because his overconfidence causes him to rest, while the determined tortoise slowly but surely walks past him and crosses the finish line.

Now, imagine a version of the story in which the hare takes off running at lightning speed, the second the starting gun sounds, but he is headed in the wrong direction. In his desire to be fastest, he fails to analyze the route and winds up running away from the finish line. Meanwhile, the intrepid tortoise makes sure he knows where he's headed, takes time to map out his route, then sets off at a deliberate pace, which allows him to deal with obstacles in the road.

By the time the hare realizes his mistake, he has gone so far in the wrong direction that he has no hope of catching the tortoise. In the end, the tortoise crosses the finish line first and wins the race.

So, what's the point of this story? Am I encouraging you to move as slowly as a tortoise in your marketing initiatives?

Not at all. Actually, I am encouraging you to take a more thoughtful approach to marketing—and any business decision, really. Before you pull the trigger, ensure that your initiatives make strategic sense. Otherwise, all the haste in the world will amount to wasted effort.

Put simply, strategy comes before execution.

Figure out your strategy before implementing tactics. Make sure the direction you're heading will take you where you need to go. To help you with this, we turn once again to the Customer Journey Infinity Loop. Place the customer directly in front of you, in all of your strategizing, to ensure that any decision will resonate with them.

BUYER'S JOURNEY—CUSTOMER LOOP

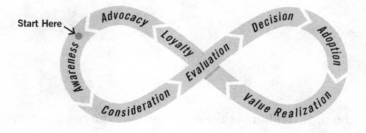

Touching, Nurturing, and Serving Prospects and Customers at Each Step

Amazon CEO, Jeff Bezos, famously leaves one empty chair in his conference rooms—a chair which is intended to represent The Customer. As he likes to say, "Start with the customer and work backward." Of course, he applies this to far more than just marketing. The Customer stays front of mind, when discussing finances, IT, or just about anything else, and the empty chair provides a constant reminder, for all in attendance, of the central focus of every decision.

FIRST IS NOT ALWAYS BEST

Customers don't necessarily care which company is first to market. Consider the fact that Google Wallet—later called Google Pay—became available in May of 2011, while Apple Pay didn't hit the market until October of 2014, three years later. Despite this, Apple Pay has twice the market share of Google Pay among the top one million websites.

MARKET SHARE BY TOP WEBSITES

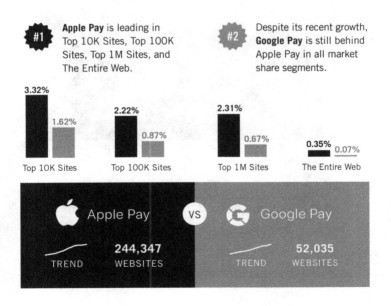

How can that be? Google Pay was a revolutionary product that made life easier for customers, and it was created and released by one of the largest companies in the world. How did Apple Pay so handily beat it, even though Apple's version lagged behind by three years?

It's all the more incredible when you consider the fact that Android phones have 75 percent of the mobile phone market. There are three times as many Android phones on the market as iPhones, and still, Apple Pay managed to become twice as popular as its competitor that had a three-year head start.

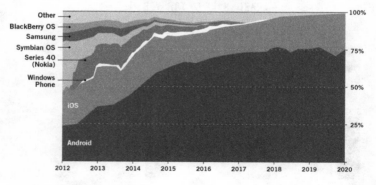

MOBILE OPERATING SYSTEMS' MARKET SHARE WORLDWIDE
FROM JANUARY 2012 TO JULY 2020

What did Apple do right with their pay service? Simple: they released it after they helped create an ecosystem to support mobile payments rather than rushing to be first. This enabled Apple to create a more complete product, and it also enabled them to time the release for when the market was better suited to accept this service. They spent time working out the kinks and, more importantly, invested in making sure a wide variety of merchants would be willing and able to accept Apple Pay from customers.

For those of you who remember physics, it's all about velocity rather than speed. Velocity is defined as speed plus direction. Instead of just trying to move as fast as possible, think about the direction you want to go and the destination you're trying to reach.

Instead of "festina lente," it might be more helpful to follow "festina ad directio" (make haste with direction). Once you are sure of the direction you need to take to get to your goal, move at a pace that suits you and your organization.

CHAPTER EIGHT

QUANTITY OVER QUALITY (IN RESEARCH)

Maybe you've had an experience like this: you eat at a restaurant, and after the meal, the server provides you with a card that has a website address on it.

"Please go online and fill out a brief survey about your experience at our restaurant this evening," she says. "In return, we will send you a coupon for a free appetizer the next time you come in."

A free appetizer sounds like a good deal, so once you arrive back home, you open the browser on your phone and navigate to the website, where you are most likely presented with a fairly lengthy survey, which will probably take longer to complete than the time you might take to enjoy that free appetizer in the future.

The survey will surely ask you numerous questions like the following: How clean was the restaurant? Did you enjoy the atmosphere? How friendly was the server? Was your order correct? How satisfied were you with the food? Was there anything we could have done better? Would you recommend this restaurant to a friend? If not, why? All of these questions will require you to provide ratings on a seven- or eleven-point scale.

Honestly, are you going to pour your heart into answering these questions? Probably not. It's more likely you will rush through them, skimming the questions and providing hasty answers with little thought or truth. If it wasn't for the free appetizer coupon at the end, you might not even complete the survey.

At the end of the quarter, the restaurant company may have received thousands of completed surveys, but how much have they really learned? Probably not much. Can they be confident that their "statistically significant" sample reflects their customers' true perceptions, opinions, and behaviors (other than that they all seem to want a free appetizer)?

I will share another well-known story from a very well-known company.

Procter & Gamble is a massive, multinational Fortune 500

company. In 2020 alone, they made a little more than $70 billion in revenue, so it's not a big deal for them to spend millions of dollars on customer research. They can easily produce an entire library of responses to customer surveys, if they so choose. Surveying 10,000 potential customers will not put a dent in Procter & Gamble's marketing budget, and it's often what they do.

But Procter & Gamble ran into trouble when they launched Febreze, their odor-eliminating fabric refresher. Initially, they positioned the product as a solution for various common household odors, such as pets and smoke. Customer response in the marketplace was tepid at best.

As reported in the New York Times, "Ads were put in heavy rotation. Then the marketers sat back, anticipating how they would spend their bonuses. A week passed. Then two. A month. Two months. Sales started small and got smaller. Febreze was a dud."[6]

Baffled P&G marketers decided to conduct in-depth conversations with target customers to figure out what they'd done wrong. For one of these conversations, they visited a woman at her home, just outside of Phoenix, Arizona. Her house was tidy and well-organized, but P&G's marketing team noticed that she owned nine cats. When they entered the living room, where most of the animals hung out, the stench was overpowering.

Suppressing his gag reflex, one of the team members asked the woman, "What do you do about the cat smell?"

She replied, "Oh, that's not a problem. They hardly smell at all."

The marketing team encountered similar smelly situations in other customer homes. Some smelled like old food, others like garbage or dogs or musty furniture. However, the homeowners didn't smell the bad odors, in their own homes, because they'd become used to them.

The experience was eye-opening (or shall we say "nose-opening?") for the marketing team. The researchers realized people didn't think they needed Febreze, because they believed their own homes smelled just fine. As far as they could tell, Febreze was a solution to a problem they personally didn't have.

After all, who was going to tell them? If you invite friends over, they're not going to say, "Wow, your house smells like garbage. Why don't you spray something to mask that stench before inviting people over? I saw an ad for this thing called Febreze. You really need it."

These few engaging and rich conversations helped the P&G team place their finger on the problem they had with Febreze's positioning. The solution to this problem was revealed in a similar conversation with another customer, who was actually using Febreze all the time.

During the conversation, she told them, "I don't really use Febreze for specific smells. I use it for normal cleaning—a couple of sprays when I'm done in a room." They followed her around the house and observed her cleaning routine. She would sweep, vacuum, mop, and then spray Febreze as a finishing touch. She explained that it felt like a mini-celebration whenever she'd finished a room.

It was a lightbulb moment for the P&G marketing team. They realized they needed to reposition Febreze not as a solution to a problem but as a perfect addition to a normal cleaning routine, something to top it off, like a cherry on a cupcake to celebrate success. They created ads with the new messaging, and within two months, sales doubled. Within a year, Febreze had brought in $230 million in revenue.

THE POWER OF A CONVERSATION

What's the common thread linking these stories? When it comes to customer insight, the quality of conversation and dialogue matters far more than quantity. Getting a handful of customers to speak, deeply and honestly, is far more helpful than simply accumulating hundreds or thousands of shallow survey answers. You will recall, this is exactly how I learned about Indian truck drivers' perception of seat belts back in the 1980s. This valuable insight came from a single face-to-face conversation.

Focus on having a few rich, engaging conversations with individuals in your target audience. This will provide more meaningful and actionable insights. And quite likely, it will cost you much less than the hundreds of surveys you were considering.

To make the most of these conversations, I recommend the following approach: first, make it feel like a conversation rather than an interview. Instead of bringing a questionnaire, prepare a list of topics (listening points) you want to cover during the conversation. Don't read them off the page. Commit them to memory, and use them to guide the conversation in a way that feels natural. It should feel like a free-flowing discussion for the customer. That's how you get people to open up.

Second, begin the conversation with a few general questions about the customer. Most people like to talk about themselves. Answers to these will also help you classify your customer in specific categories that you would like to see as part of your research. These warmup questions can help get the ball rolling, but remember, this is not a question-and-answer session. Keep the scope of your questions broad and open-ended, so the interviewee always views it as a conversation.

Third, don't assume you have to bribe someone in order to have a conversation. Believe it or not, most people want to talk about their experiences with a product or service. They might even feel flattered that you're taking the time to talk to them about it.

Fourth, I recommend having conversations with five or six people—just a handful—certainly no more than ten, in any specific target group or for any particular product category. Even with ten, you may learn enough from the first five that the latter five are simply confirming what you've already learned. The marginal incremental value of conversations gets smaller and smaller the more conversations you have.

Fifth, focus on listening rather than talking. Instead of thinking about what your next question is going to be, pay attention to what the person you're speaking with is saying. Don't ask leading questions (e.g., "How angry did you feel when the product stopped working?") or attempt to embed an expected answer into the conversation. You want honest, heartfelt, and thoughtful opinions of their actual experience. Remember, listening isn't a passive activity. Once the person you're speaking with has expressed their opinion, summarize it to them to ensure you've understood it correctly.

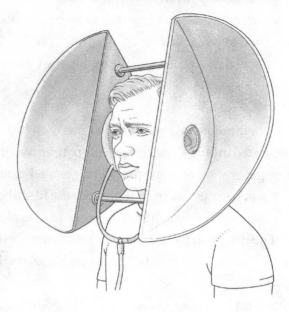

Sixth, if possible, conduct these conversations face-to-face or, at least, through video chat. Talking over the phone creates distance that will make it more difficult to build the rapport and trust essential to getting the richness of responses you are seeking.

Seventh, control your own responses and reactions. You are there to learn from the customer, not to sell, educate, or debate. If it becomes clear that the customer misused the product, refrain from correcting them right then and there. If you feel qualified to advise the customer, do so as an aside, as you are leaving. Alternatively, take that information back to your service and design teams, and get them to make improvements to your product or messaging, so customers in the future won't misuse the product in a similar way.

Lastly, don't feel compelled to fill any awkward silences. Embrace them. Natural, free-flowing conversations have occasional awkward silences; indeed, the customer may use the pause to relax and reflect on some valuable detail or emotional nuance that you missed earlier.

SPEND TIME WITH CUSTOMERS

When I worked for Cummins, a multinational corporation that primarily manufactures engines and generators, we used to conduct product clinics, where we would spend time with customers as they used our products. From time to time, the marketing, engineering, and sales teams would get together and spend the day with an actual customer.

We called it: "A Day in the Life of a Customer."

We would hang out with them and observe how they used our product. Along the way, we might chat, but mostly we just observed and listened.

Afterward, our cross-functional teams would get together

and discuss what we'd learned, from spending the time with customers, looking for ways to improve the customer experience or the product itself. We learned far more from the time we spent with those individual customers than we ever learned from conducting largescale surveys.

Don't assume that more is better when getting customer feedback. For best results, focus on rich and engaging interactions with a few people rather than casting your net as widely as possible.

PART THREE

SMALL-M MARKETING

CHAPTER NINE

SOCIAL DISTANCING IN SOCIAL MEDIA

As a professor, I often present my students with a real product from a make-believe company and ask them to develop a business strategy and a marketing plan for it. They then have five minutes to present these to the class. Often, in the first iteration of their plan, they confidently share that they will "use social media to do their marketing." And that's it. That's the entirety of their marketing plan. They quickly realize that this simplistic recommendation is the shortest way to an F.

Flooding social media with information about your product is not good marketing, though it is an all-too-common approach that companies take. So many business leaders think that if they post something about their product on

Facebook, Instagram, and Twitter, every single day, eventually they'll gain traction. That becomes the core and extent of their marketing plan.

Social media platforms are nothing more than channels you can use to get your message out. Figuring out which channels you're going to use in your marketing only answers about 5 percent of the questions you need to ask. Indeed, without the right positioning and messaging, it might be a complete waste of time and money.

Who are you going to target? What's your positioning? What's your messaging? What will you present at each stage of the customer journey? What information will you include in your marketing at each of these stages? These are the kinds of questions you have to answer. Once you have answers to these (and other) essential questions, you can explore your social media options and what role they might play in advancing your objectives.

IT'S NOT A SILVER BULLET

Let me be crystal clear: I am not against social media. Far from it! However, I meet too many business leaders who think social media is a silver bullet that will automatically bring amazing results. Consequently, they spend very little time or money figuring out how to use these channels effectively.

Think carefully about the customer journey before you start dumping content onto social media. Bear in mind, social media responds faster than more traditional channels. You are going to get a response within seconds, unlike something in print, which might take days or weeks. This can be either a positive or a negative, depending on how much thought you put into creating the content for social media.

Another characteristic of social media you have to keep in mind is that you have less control over it than most other media. Once you begin interacting with the public on social media, you are just one of many on the platform voicing an opinion. What you receive as feedback or response is unpredictable and may well be surprising.

If you put up a billboard that the public doesn't like, someone might eventually climb up there and spray graffiti on it. If they don't like your print ad, they might write angry letters to the editor. However, social media feedback begins, as soon as you post, and it may come in a tidal wave that overwhelms you. You can exert a small measure of control, but for the most part, it's a freewheeling experience. If you're not ready for it, your brand, product, or service may suffer.

Let's look at a few examples of companies that learned this lesson the hard way.

THE PERILS OF SOCIAL MEDIA MARKETING

PROMOTING "CLEAN" OR RACIST/TONE-DEAF ADVERTISING?

In 2017, Unilever ran a four-panel ad for their Dove soap brand on Facebook, which resulted in a significant backlash. In the first two panels, an African American woman is seen removing her shirt. In the third and fourth panels, after stripping off her shirt, she appears to have transformed into a white woman.

According to a Dove spokeswoman, the ad "was intended to convey that Dove Body Wash is for every woman and be a celebration of diversity." However, to the general public, it seemed to convey the idea that light skin equals cleanliness. The outcry on social media was swift and brutal, and the brand was tainted with accusations of tone-deafness at best, and overt racism at worst.[7]

The company swiftly apologized and pulled the ad, but because of the nature of social media, the conversation was out of their hands by that point. The general public shaped the debate, and Unilever was essentially at their mercy.

This isn't the only time a major company inadvertently conveyed a racist message in their social media ads. In 2020, Volkswagen posted a video on Instagram for their Golf 8 compact car. In the ad, a giant white hand is seen pushing a black man away from a parked Golf 8 and flicking him through the open door of a restaurant. A sign above the door identifies the restaurant as Petit Colon, which is French for "Little Colonist."

The public was understandably shocked and baffled by the message. What was Volkswagen trying to convey with this ad? In response to the outrage, Head of Sales and Marketing, Jürgen Stackmann, gave no excuses or explanations. Appropriately, he simply apologized by saying, "On behalf of Volkswagen AG, we apologize to the public at large for this film. And we apologize in particular to those who feel personally hurt by the racist content because of their own history."[8]

Similarly, in 2019, Burger King in New Zealand got in trouble for posting an ad on Instagram for a Vietnamese-themed sandwich, which featured a white woman feeding the sandwich to an Asian man, using comically oversized chopsticks. A catchphrase above the video read, "Take your taste buds all the way to Ho Chi Minh City." The backlash was immediate, and the fast-food chain quickly deleted the video, but not before it had racked up 2.7 million views and garnered widespread derision and thousands of angry comments for the company.[9]

Of course, even hastily deleted social media posts live on. You can probably still find this deleted Burger King ad all over the internet. The internet never forgets!

Examples like these go on and on. If you get your messaging wrong on social media, the backlash can begin almost instantly. If you're not ready to handle it, you might wind up damaging your brand, even with the best of intentions.

Most of these examples seem so obviously dumb in hindsight. So, why do these kinds of social media blunders happen so frequently and to the best of companies?

Think about it: as CEO, you have probably asked your marketing team to just get some marketing material out there, as quickly as possible, so that people will notice and talk about your company. To an average or inexperienced marketer, this is an open invitation to create something fast, and social media offers a quick way to check the box and get the CEO off marketing's back. For reasons illustrated above, this is incredibly dangerous because it can be done thoughtlessly, with unintended consequences.

I strongly encourage you to give yourself and your marketing team the space to think carefully about your targeting, positioning, and messaging, before you publish content on any platform, including social media platforms. If you'll pardon the pun, you need to socially distance from social media first, because once you post, the conversation is largely out of your hands.

Far from being a silver bullet, social media marketing requires careful consideration and smart planning. Used wisely, it can become an essential part of an effective marketing plan.

CHAPTER TEN

LIKES AND FOLLOWERS

The Beatles famously sang, "Can't buy me love." But many companies are attempting to do exactly that, all the time. They sink large amounts of money into buying likes and followers for their various social media accounts. It seems to make sense. After all, it's better to have more likes and followers, and the fastest way to achieve that is to buy them. Right?

The problem is that, quite simply, the appearance of customer engagement is not customer engagement.

Fake likes are just that: fake. Indeed, the only person who profits, when you pay for likes and followers, is the guy running the shady company that sold those likes to you in the first place. Some company leaders believe they are paying for actual likes, as if the provider were a middleman making contact with actual people. In reality, most of these likes come from fake accounts created by the provider. It's a disreputable industry, operating on the edge of legality, and no respectable business should have anything to do with it.

So, what's the allure of easy likes?

There are an estimated 3.6 billion people on social media, and that number is projected to increase to 4.4 billion by 2025. That's half the population of the human race! People of all ages, from young children to seniors in their eighties and nineties, are active on various platforms.

According to research, in the US alone, individuals spend an average of one hour and fifty-seven minutes every day on social media. These statistics will come as no surprise to anyone who has a teenager at home. What may come as a surprise, though, is that this number doesn't even place the United States at the top of the list for social media usage. The top spot belongs to the Philippines, where people spend more than four hours per day on social media!

With such a massive audience apparently at your fingertips, it's easy to see the allure of grabbing your piece of the social media action. Spending a few thousand dollars to get tens of thousands—or even hundreds of thousands—of likes and followers can seem like an easy way in. But this is not social media marketing. It's the modern-day version of fool's gold, and should be treated with equal skepticism.

As marketing expert Guy Kawasaki famously said, "There are two types of people on social media: people who want more followers, and liars."

The problem with buying artificial likes and followers is that they don't really drive business. It might be exciting to see big numbers after your posts, but you're not creating actual engagement. Indeed, in terms of actual impact on your bottom line, it's more effective to have a hundred real followers who are actively engaged than 10,000 phony followers who just pad the numbers.

Fake followers don't produce leads, because no fake account is ever going to buy from you. Fake followers don't visit your website. Furthermore, if they're not actively engaging with you, they don't really encourage real people to pay attention. You might think that boosting your likes will have a trickle-down effect, by encouraging the social media algorithm to put your content in front of more people, but it could have the opposite effect.

When you have a social media account that is padded with thousands of fake followers and likes, your engagement level, as a percentage of those followers, is going to tank. Fake people aren't clicking on links or posting comments.

They're not actively engaging with your company, products, or services. Think about it. What does it look like when you've got 100,000 followers but none of them ever have anything to say to you? Yes, 100,000 people liked your post, but none of them are engaging in a conversation with you. That's going to do more harm than good, because when your engagement score drops, your social media account ranking will drop along with it.

DON'T INVEST IN AN ILLUSION

Sometimes, companies will go a step further. Beyond buying likes and followers, they will pay one of these shady companies to actually make content posts for them, too. These tend to be spam, or at least low-quality posts, that eventually drive away the company's few real customers. What's the point of getting 10,000 fake people to like your spam posts, when the 200 real, live customers get annoyed and tune you out?

It's a dangerous game. Besides driving away the small group of followers that makes the biggest impact on your bottom line, you might also get caught. People are more concerned about internet privacy than ever before, which has put increasing pressure on social media companies like Facebook and Twitter. The noose is going to tighten for fake accounts, fake followers, and fake likes. You don't want to find your legitimate business in the crosshairs, just because you bought a bit of social media response. It's not worth the risk to your reputation.

In terms of real dollars and cents, the cost of fake likes might be low, but don't forget the opportunity cost. You can spend a thousand dollars to get 100,000 easy, fake followers, which will make almost no impact on your bottom line. Or, you can focus your time and money on earning 5,000 real, live followers, who will engage with you and build your online reputation. Unfortunately, when companies decide to do the former, they tend to neglect the latter.

Take all of that money you would invest in fake likes, and instead spend it on creating deeper engagement and converting real customers into brand advocates. Use the customer journey loop to engage with them every step of the way. Just a handful of people with a positive view of your company is worth all the fake followers in the world. Beyond likes, they are the ones who will actually comment, discuss, and praise your brand, products, and services.

THE POWER OF MEETING REAL PEOPLE

When I worked with a software company called iTexico, we decided to hold annual customer councils to deepen our engagement with our customers and get honest feedback, directly from them.

We invited them to Guadalajara, Mexico, to visit the operations and meet with the management and engineers working on their projects. It was an opportunity for the company to have face-to-face conversations with its customers, in both business conference rooms as well as social settings, as we wined and dined together.

As valuable as these interactions were, an even greater value came out of inviting prospective customers to these same customer councils. Honest conversations between prospective customers and current customers had a powerful impact. These conversations carried far more weight and credibility than anything the company might say, or even demonstrate.

Letting prospective customers interact with current customers provided opportunities for unrehearsed, authentic sharing of experiences, and customer testimonials that no conventional marketing or CEO-talk could ever achieve. We found that nearly 80 percent of our prospective customer guests became actual iTexico customers after attending these customer councils.

That's the power of real, authentic, and live engagement. Don't waste a penny on fake likes or make-believe followers. These are exactly the kind of lies you want to avoid.

CHAPTER ELEVEN

MORE TOOLS, LESS MASTERY

The world of marketing technology continues to grow exponentially, year after year. According to an article by marketing expert Scott Brinker, the marketing technology (MarTech) landscape grew by 13.6 percent in 2020. There are now 8,000 MarTech solutions available.[10] The graphic visualization of this is truly eye-straining. It would make a good eye chart for testing your vision at the optometrist's office.

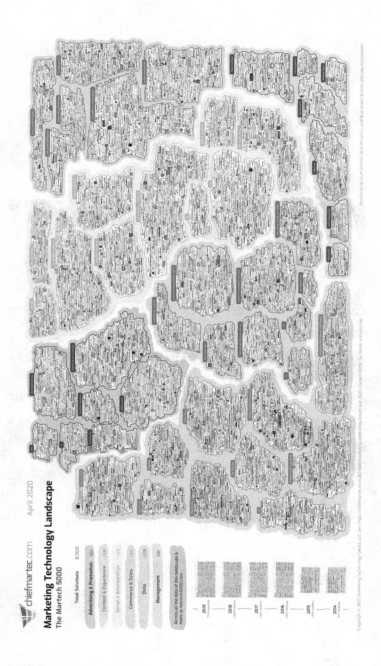

Marketing Technology Landscape
The Martech 5000

You might wonder why people keep creating new marketing products and tools, when the marketplace is already absurdly overloaded. The explanation given is generally some version or combination of the following:

- none of the existing solutions work.
- our product is the one you've been waiting for.
- all other products have some weakness or failing that we have covered in our new product.

After providing this explanation, the company will likely present you with a matrix full of checkmarks next to their product, contrasted with empty boxes by their competitors' offerings.

Even smart people buy into this hype, because they've had disappointing results with the previous MarTech products they've used.

Here's the truth, plain and simple: you probably don't need another tool. All you need to do is learn how to use the ones you've already got!

Think about it like this: let's say that, during the COVID-19 lockdown, you went ahead and bought a treadmill to replace the gym you couldn't go to. After six months of occasional use, you are not happy with the results, so you decide to buy an elliptical machine to replace your treadmill.

After another few months of occasional use, the elliptical machine yields no better results. This cycle repeats through the course of a few more purchases and many more disappointing months. What's going on here? Are these exercise tools no good, or are you not using them properly?

Similarly, if you're failing to get the most out of your current MarTech tools, then the latest, shiniest tool probably won't work for you either. I see so many CEOs hopping from one tool to the next, spending a whole lot of money along the way, in hopes that one of them will eventually perform magic.

A surgeon's instruments can save a patient's life, but not if they are placed in the hands of an untrained teenager with no medical knowledge. The tools themselves don't save lives—the surgeon's expertise in using them does.

SELECTING THE RIGHT MARTECH TOOLS

When it comes to choosing marketing technology tools for your company, don't chase after the shiniest new option. The fact that a tool is new doesn't necessarily mean that it will be the best option for meeting your needs. All too often, MarTech tools follow Gartner's famous hype cycle.

GARTNER HYPE CYCLE FOR DIGITAL MARKETING AND ADVERTISING, 2019

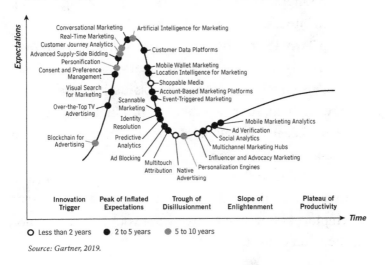

Source: Gartner, 2019.

Initially, everyone is excited about this cutting-edge tool and all the things it can do, anticipating massive growth and an increase in profitability at warp speed. Market buzz is created and hyped. The product is pumped up, creating rising expectations. Eventually, however, team members begin to encounter some practical difficulties in using the tool, and the excitement starts to fade. Ultimately, it becomes another ho-hum product.

This is the time when many fall into the trap of thinking, "Now it's time to find another shiny, new marketing tool."

Instead, I recommend the following four-step process:

- Step One: identify your marketing needs, grouping them into must-haves and nice-to-haves.
- Step Two: look at possible options, focusing on MarTech tools that are designed to meet your specific needs. Don't become enamored with tools just because they're new. Indeed, more established products might work better, because developers have had time to refine them and make improvements.
- Step Three: make sure your company is prepared to invest the time and money necessary to train your employees how to effectively use your new tool. If not, then don't buy it!

TOOLS WITHOUT USER TRAINING

- Step Four: look for established tools that have gone through the crescendo and come out on the other side intact. They've moved beyond hype, beyond difficulties, to the real meat and potatoes of what the product has to offer. A MarTech tool that has lasted through this cycle has proved itself in the trenches. Also, there are going to be more resources for learning how to make the most of it.

Don't obsess over marketing tech selection too much. Most MarTech tools will be just fine for what you need to do. Even though there are a variety of hammers at your local hardware store, most of them are perfectly suitable for driving in nails, as long as you use them correctly. You don't have to get the shiniest or the most expensive one to drive nails and hang your pictures around the house.

As long as you invest the time and money to learn the tool and train your employees, you're going to get your money's worth out of it. Be wary of new-tool hype, and don't buy into the idea that some fancy tool is going to take the place of good training and hard work.

CHAPTER TWELVE

QUANTITY OVER QUALITY (IN TACTICS)

A company in Southern California hired me as a fractional CMO for a project that was intended to last six to nine months. I scheduled a kickoff meeting onsite. The CEO, in his well-intentioned enthusiasm, decided to go above and beyond my agenda by turning the meeting into a two-hour brainstorming session. It went something like this: "Today, we're going to brainstorm all of the things we can do to jumpstart marketing at our company," he announced.

He then proceeded to go around the room and have each person share their own laundry list of ideas.

"Let's do trade shows!"

"Let's send out an email blast!"

"Let's create fun videos on Instagram!"

"Let's send coupons by snail mail!"

Like any good brainstorming session, people mentioned anything that came to mind. When I was able to get a word in edgewise, I asked, "Why are we doing this at the kickoff meeting?"

"I just want to get everything out on the table," the CEO replied.

This went on for two full hours. At the end of it, we had an enormous list of ideas that were all over the map.

When we finished, I took the CEO aside. "If you think great marketing comes from creating a laundry list of every possible thing that could be called marketing, then you don't need to spend money on me," I told him. "You can buy a marketing how-to book on Amazon for less than twenty bucks, and it will give you what you're looking for."

WHAT NOT TO DO

Great marketing is knowing what to do, when, and how to do it, but just as importantly, it's knowing what not to do. Creating a laundry list of marketing tactics is simple enough, but how do you know which things to take off of that list?

If you're not getting good results from your marketing efforts, you probably don't need more tactics; you need better tactics and, perhaps, even a decent strategy upon which these tactics are premised. Simply doing more things rarely helps. A single marketing idea, based on solid reasoning, will do more for you than trying twenty or thirty different things in a scattershot approach.

If you just want to flood the brains of your team with a bunch of different marketing ideas, refer back to our small-m marketing chart in Chapter One. I have provided a dozen ideas right there.

This is a scenario that almost every marketing person will encounter at some point, regardless of the size of the company they work for or their position in the hierarchy. At some point, leaders will approach them wanting more marketing. Suddenly, the team is being pressured to put out more emails, create more advertising, and tweet more often.

More marketing means more sales, right? So, get to work!

Under this kind of pressure, the marketing team will come

up with some kind of list of incremental things they will do to satisfy the CEO. They'll decide to pay for 1,000 more subscribers and put out a huge email blast. The CEO will likely be impressed that the email list increased by 50 percent and figure the marketing team really took the ball and ran with it.

In the short term, the CEO and leadership are happy, and the pressure on the marketing team eases. However, in most instances, nothing of any real substance is achieved, except wasted time and money.

As one CEO friend of mine put it, "In marketing, people mistake motion for movement." You want movement, not motion.

Let me make this point with a chart of the reasons customers break up with brands. As this chart clearly demonstrates, one of the primary reasons customers break up with brands is receiving too much marketing content. Keep this chart in mind before you decide to blast your customers with yet another email that consists of recycled content.

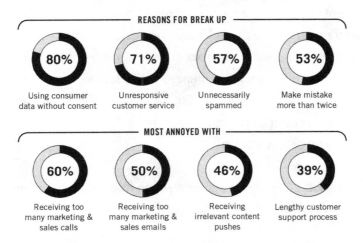

WHY DO CONSUMERS BREAK UP WITH BRANDS?
TOP REASONS FOR CONSUMERS TO SHUN BRANDS AND MOST DISLIKED BEHAVIORS

REASONS FOR BREAK UP

80% Using consumer data without consent

71% Unresponsive customer service

57% Unnecessarily spammed

53% Make mistake more than twice

MOST ANNOYED WITH

60% Receiving too many marketing & sales calls

50% Receiving too many marketing & sales emails

46% Receiving irrelevant content pushes

39% Lengthy customer support process

Base: 20,000 consumers in 20 countries across Europe, Asia, Latin America, the Middle East and North America
Source: SAP Hybris © StatistaCharts

Still, the more-marketing mantra makes sense to many business leaders. They figure if they're getting a little bit of engagement from sending out an email once a month, they'll get a lot more if they send an email out twice a month. You can see the pseudo-logic behind this kind of thinking: if a little action brings a little return, then a lot of action will bring a lot of return.

It's simply not true, though. Higher quality marketing will produce vastly better results than a greater quantity of marketing. Don't confuse bigness with greatness.

Let's examine this from another angle, one that is usually very close to every CEO's heart: lead generation.

According to the marketing firm Sirius Decisions, less than 1 percent of leads are converted into actual sales. This means that if you have a hundred leads, one of them might result in a sale. Why is the number so low? In my opinion, it's because people have a very generous and loose idea of what constitutes a lead. A person isn't a lead just because they receive an email from your company, look at a brochure, or endure an online commercial.

If you want to improve your conversion rate, produce higher quality leads.

Imagine if your conversion rate was 10 percent instead of 1 percent. You'd need fewer leads and still increase sales; in other words, less effort for higher revenue.

In 2016 Accenture conducted a study that revealed that fewer than 18 percent of the people who are contacted by companies are actually in the market for the product or service being offered.[11] Think of that. It means 82 percent of the people in your marketing campaign are a waste of time.

They're not in the market for your product, no matter how much you pester them about it. Unless you are selling impulse purchase items (like a pack of chewing gum you might pick up while waiting at the checkout line), the spray-and-pray marketing method is never going to convert them to sales.

FOCUSED ON THE WRONG THINGS

As you can see in the following chart, produced by ANNU-ITAS in 2019, 80 percent of nonmarketing and non-sales business leaders, and a whopping 95 percent of sales leaders, believe that marketing is focused on the wrong metrics.

TODAY'S REALITY—LACK OF ALIGNED SUCCESS METRICS

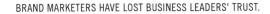

BRAND MARKETERS HAVE LOST BUSINESS LEADERS' TRUST.

80% of non-marketing/non-sales business leaders with a Brand-Focused CMO think that marketing is focused on the wrong metrics.
Brand, PR, and Product-focused

95% of sales leaders with a Brand-Focused CMO think that marketing is focused on the wrong metrics.
Demand, Sales, and Revenue-focused

Source: ANNUITAS, 2019 Demand Marketing Performance Study

Put more bluntly, a vast majority of leaders believe marketers are just off in the weeds, working on the wrong things for the wrong reasons. This is incredibly discouraging. In light of this overwhelmingly negative view, why would anyone want to become a marketer?

To add insult to injury, marketing research company Forrester found that digital-buyer experience exceeds customer expectations only 7 percent of the time. Put another way, more than nine times out of ten, people have an experience that is as bad, or worse, than they expected.

What do these statistics indicate? I don't know about you, but to me, as a marketer (and a consumer of marketing in my personal life), this focus on quantity over quality in marketing tactics is having a detrimental effect. The perception is that marketers are just dumping all kinds of meaningless content that provides little positive value out there.

My recommendation? Stop the spray-and-pray approach. Do less marketing, while demanding and expecting more out of marketing.

That's right. Focus on creating higher-quality marketing content rather than trying to do as much as possible. Target higher-quality leads, with the well-targeted positioning that is reflected in well-timed, crisp, and appropriate messaging.

Once again, look at the customer journey loop, consider each step of that journey, and make smart, tactical decisions for reaching the right people, at the right time, with the information they most need in a manner they are more likely to accept. This requires possessing greater insights about your customers and marketplace, more preparation time, and more careful consideration and planning, but the end result will be well worth it.

CHAPTER THIRTEEN

RANDOM ACTS OF MARKETING

I had an epiphany when I discovered the impact of random acts in the business world. It came to me, in a charming and allegorical manner, when I was the global CMO of Kodak Health Imaging, a $3+ billion business at the time.

We were at an annual, weeklong global leadership forum, during which the top 250 leaders from around the world gathered at corporate headquarters to exchange ideas, learn new things, and have a little fun. At this particular year's event, the highlight was a learning session run by a music conductor named Roger Nierenberg.

After an illustrious career as music conductor of various orchestras, Nierenberg leads a business leadership organization called The Music Paradigm. His four-hour program on leadership used music as a metaphor for many of the challenges and choices faced by business leaders. He illustrated this by using the orchestra and his own role as conductor.

For me, this program was particularly eye-opening on multiple levels. I grew up loving rock and roll and didn't develop an ear for classical music until later in life. Even then, I often wondered about the role of the conductor. As far as I could tell, all they did was swing a stick to the beat, as if they were simply trying to keep up with the music, while the musicians did all of the hard, creative work.

The musicians at the event that day were clearly world-class performers. This became apparent, as we listened, mesmerized, to the overture from Mozart's The Magic Flute. After conducting for about seven minutes, Mr. Nierenberg paused and suggested that we experiment a little bit. He asked the orchestra to replay the same piece again, but this time, he walked into the audience and took a seat with us.

After a few moments of hesitation and looking at one another for a start cue, the orchestra started playing once again. For the first minute or so, everything seemed just fine. But soon, even those of us with untrained ears in the audience noticed that the music started to drift a little bit. Then it began falling apart. In less than three minutes, many of the musicians were openly expressing their own frustration—some at themselves, but mostly at their colleagues. Within about five minutes, the music descended into a complete mess, and the orchestra decided to stop playing—largely out of the musicians' own embarrassment, but also to save us from what may be described as a chaotic cacophony.

CONDUCTING YOUR MARKETING SYMPHONY

What does this have to do with marketing? The first time the orchestra played The Magic Flute, it sounded as good as Mozart intended it to. Every note from every instrument came together to form the backdrop and introduction to a signature piece of music that Mozart composed the year he died.

However, in the second playing of the same piece, things didn't go so well. There was no magic in this rendering of The Magic Flute. Why? Not because any of the musicians played poorly, or with any less enthusiasm, but rather due to a lack of the coordination and cohesion that is critical in any multi-instrument composition. The musicians struggled to deliver the cohesive whole, even though each one of them did a masterful job. Overall, the impact of playing without a conductor was a big mess.

Similarly, your marketing department may be doing many things well. You may have created compelling advertisements. Your billboards might look amazing. You're getting some engagement on social media. You're attending trade shows. However, if each of these marketing elements is being executed without a well-thought-out and cohesive strategy, they will be less than fully productive and can actually begin to counteract each other. When that happens, you may wind up with a bunch of random acts of marketing, which may look great individually, but together, have a suboptimal or even a negative return on your total investment.

Just as these world-class musicians, with their music sheets in front of them, managed to create a cacophony out of a beautiful piece of music, when left to run in an uncoordinated manner, your best marketing programs could create chaos. You, or someone in your organization, needs to serve as the conductor of your marketing orchestra so the whole piece comes out sounding great.

Even the best musicians (read marketers), playing the best instruments (read executing marketing tactics well), will be ineffective unless all of the players are aligned, reading off the same music sheet and led by a conductor (read well-crafted and executed strategic plan).

TELLTALE SIGNS OF UNCOORDINATED MARKETING

Often, the negative effects of randomness are not immediately obvious. Just as the orchestra managed to sound good for the first minute or so, individual marketing programs can also appear to be effective and solid. To make matters even more confusing, each tactic can potentially deliver metrics that stand up to scrutiny by a tough CFO.

So how do you know if your business is suffering from (or about to experience) the ill effects of random acts of marketing?

The good news is that there are a few telltale signs.

First, if you have multiple marketing tactics in your budget but can't connect the dots between them, it's likely an indicator that you're conducting random acts of marketing. In other words, if you have well-defined (and well-funded) tactics but are unable to stitch them together as part of your overall strategy, you are likely doing random acts of marketing.

Second, if you're conducting brainstorming sessions, every time you miss your monthly or quarterly sales goal, so you can create laundry lists of all the possible things your team can think of—like, for instance, creating an email newsletter, getting more involved on YouTube, and mailing a coupon—without any coordinated reason for doing so, that's also a big sign. A spray-and-pray approach to marketing is inherently uncoordinated and wasteful.

Third, if you're constantly looking for new marketing tools or constantly attracted to the newest and shiniest tool, there's a good chance you lack overall cohesion in your marketing. You may be looking for a mythical silver bullet that doesn't exist.

Fourth, if you're buying leads to fill your sales funnel, rather than generating them, through a coordinated marketing effort, it's another good sign you're doing random acts of marketing.

Fifth, if you find yourself hiring and firing marketing people frequently, without having a good reason to do so other than a vague hope that, somehow, someone on a white, magical horse will appear to save the day, it's also a good sign of uncoordinated marketing efforts.

WHAT'S SO WRONG WITH RANDOM?

You might be wondering what's wrong with trying a whole bunch of different marketing techniques. Even if they're uncoordinated, a few might gain traction. As for the ones that don't work, you can dial them back.

The problem with this kind of thinking is that you won't know what's working and what's not working, so you won't know what to dial back.

Consequently, even if you experience some success, you won't know which efforts to dial back and which ones to double down on. As a result, you'll end up wasting time and money, even in the midst of success.

Another reason for avoiding randomness in your marketing finds its roots in our discussion in the previous chapter. You will recall that, statistically speaking, the average conversion rate from lead to sale is less than 1 percent. This in itself is, of course, indicative of a low quality of leads.

However, if you do root-cause analysis behind lower-quality leads, you are likely to find uncoordinated, haphazard, and random acts of marketing feeding the funnel with lower-quality leads. Thus, your desire and efforts to fill the top of your funnel are actually hurting your ultimate goal of achieving productive conversion to sales.

So, what's the solution? How can you avoid haphazard marketing?

Spend some time creating a strategic marketing plan before you get into specific marketing tactics. Once you have a strategy in place, focus on high-quality marketing, rather than trying to do as many things as possible. Keep a list of marketing ideas and tactics you are choosing not to implement. This will ensure that you are being thoughtful and honest about your planning process, as opposed to doing everything you can think of (and afford). Make sure every part of your marketing plan is pulling in the same direction.

How do you begin to create your strategic marketing plan?

First, identify your target audience.

Second, create their persona, and map out their buying journey. How do they consume information at each step of the journey? What are they looking for?

Third, focus on developing programs addressing all four Ps of marketing (product/service, price, place, and promotion) for your chosen segments and personas of your target audiences.

Fourth, build a content-generation engine that will feed into the customer journey. In other words, make sure you are creating the right kinds of content to address their questions, concerns, and needs, at various steps along their buying journey.

Fifth, establish a good lead-management process. Once you start getting leads, make sure you know who's going to handle them and how they're going to be dealt with. You don't want leads to get lost because no one takes responsibility for them, or because you lack a consistent means of responding to them.

Sixth, plan for converting your customers into your advocates. How will you leverage your success to get you more success?

Once you've followed these steps, each marketing tactic will have a purpose and rightful place in your overall strategy. You will also find that each tactic relates (or should relate) to each of the steps in the Customer Journey Infinity Loop.

Orchestrated together as part of your overall strategy, your tactics will stimulate demand, generate leads, convert them into sales, and make your loyal customers your best advocates.

PART FOUR

BIG-M + SMALL-M MARKETING

CHAPTER FOURTEEN

FAKE ROI

We are all obsessed with ROI. That's no secret. We want to make the best use of our dollars, and we believe ROI is a simple but effective way to make good business decisions. As Peter Drucker once said, "What gets measured, gets managed."

Unfortunately, we have somehow extended Peter Drucker's pithy wisdom to a false corollary of "what can't be measured is not worth managing or doing." Let me illustrate this with an example.

Driving from San Francisco to San Jose on Route 101 can take anywhere from one to three hours, depending on the time of day. Along the way, no matter which direction you're headed, you will see at least a dozen large billboards advertising the iPhone.

Most of these billboards showcase actual photographs taken by iPhone customers. They are captivating, interesting, and nice to look at during a slow drive, and they show a lot of creativity from iPhone users. They also implicitly highlight the technical capabilities of the iPhone camera and software, and its ability to make a professional photographer out of anyone.

Still, what is a data-savvy tech company like Apple doing pouring so much money into such an archaic form of communication? More pertinently, why in the world would Apple spend millions of dollars on billboard-advertising when the company almost certainly has no way to measure the ROI of these billboards? Clearly, they can't tie incremental iPhone sales to specific billboards or billboards in general.

In fact, there isn't much, if any, direct data that can be gleaned about the effectiveness of these billboards. It's not like measuring clicks on a website, after all. Despite this, Apple continues to pour money into them, using an emotional hook to appeal to their prospective customers (just as I had suggested doing in Chapter Two).

The reason Apple continues to spend millions on billboards is because they know a lot of people in their target audience will see them. Drivers spend a lot of time on Route 101, which makes these billboards prime real estate, perfect for delivering Apple's message. On top of this, the company has focused on warm and fuzzy marketing that showcases the work of their own users, which just might provide frustrated drivers a much needed and welcome distraction from staring at other people's brake lights.

In my experience, many companies would hesitate to take this apparent leap of faith without access to a specific ROI. Indeed, many businesses only feel comfortable when they can tie a specific ROI number to their marketing efforts. They insist on seeing the data before investing in anything. No data, no approval; what can't be measured shouldn't be done.

GREAT DECISIONS WITHOUT ROI? YES!

In 2019, I was hired by the CEO of a major diagnostic imaging company in California to help develop their marketing strategy and refresh their brand. They were in the process of switching to direct-to-patient marketing and wanted a new look for their outdated logo and website, to coincide with the change.

Indeed, their existing logo had been around for the entire thirty-year lifespan of the company. The CEO seemed particularly concerned about the ugly brown color of their logo, and he asked about doing research to determine which new colors should be used in the new design.

"Pick colors that look attractive and go well together," I advised him. "You don't have to spend money or time researching this. Just make sure you don't pick green."

"What's wrong with green?" he asked.

"In the last few years, green has become increasingly associated with the cannabis industry," I explained. "Look at the cannabis dispensaries across the country. Most of them have logos that are green and have some sort of a cross or emblem related to cannabis. Regardless of your personal feelings about legalized cannabis, it's not something you want your diagnostic imaging company to be confused with."

If I had been less than ethical, I could have sold them a $25,000 research project conducting massive surveys of a cross section of their target market. Instead, I backed up my recommendation by simply Googling images of marijuana-related company logos.

Voila! The search results were a sea of green. My point was made, and the company saved a bunch of time and money. A less confident marketer might have wanted the data to justify his advice, but it wouldn't have been worth the expense.

To make a long story short, the CEO decided to trust my

judgment. He asked me to share my thoughts with the board of directors, and they agreed. They settled on a nice logo with no green in it, and the refresh of their brand was successful, without the unnecessary expense of data-seeking research.

Let's put all of this together.

To start, Apple continues to spend millions on its billboards on Route 101, because it knows that traffic is only getting worse each day, which means their billboards gain ever-increasing exposure to the technophile audience living and working in the Bay Area. Why wouldn't Apple want to impress all of these people with their latest products? Even if the ROI can't be measured, the number of eyeballs being exposed to their billboards can be. That is the justification for their spending.

Similarly, even though I didn't provide my client with any negative ROI that might result from using green in their new logo, I was able to justify my advice. I provided no ROI, but my good judgment, supported with reason, logic, and visual evidence, made the point.

So why does this obsession with ROI exist in so many companies? And is it really such a bad thing?

I'll answer the second question first. In my opinion, ROI has become just another aspect of a marketing security blanket that people want to hide behind when making decisions. How did it get to this point?

For the most part, it's the result of marketing teams fighting for a piece of the pie. Leaders sit around a table and debate how they're going to spend their money. As part of this, the CMO has to justify their expenditures on various marketing campaigns.

The engineer's pitch is a lot easier: "Give me a million dollars, and my team will build a new product."

That makes sense. It's tangible. The money spent directly connects to a tangible outcome.

Then the CMO raises his hands and says, "I want to spend a million dollars on billboards on Route 101." It's natural for the CFO to wonder if they would be flushing that money down the proverbial toilet. Consequently, marketers have often felt compelled to justify their expenditures in some direct way in order to receive the money they need to fund their efforts. The easiest way to do that is to tie a specific ROI to every marketing campaign. It's easier for decision makers to commit when the math is clear.

As a result, ROI has become the way in which every marketing project is measured. The only problem is that some of the most impactful marketing campaigns can't be readily tied to a clear ROI. In those instances, marketers are often tempted to make up numbers or, worse, to ignore great marketing ideas altogether, simply because there aren't ROI numbers to justify them.

ROI numbers sound attractive and can easily be plugged into a spreadsheet. Unfortunately, it's an unhealthy practice, which can become ingrained in the company. Expected return is now connected to every single marketing effort.

Today, the business of marketing has essentially become the CMO telling the CEO, "If we spend X amount of money on Marketing Project A, over the next twelve months, your revenue will increase by X amount." This kind of marketing ROI (mROI) gets forced into everything.

There are a few issues with this approach, demonstrated with a simple example. Let's say your annual revenue is $10 million, with a contribution margin of 33 percent. In working with your CMO, you've come up with a growth plan to take your revenue to $13 million the following year. Your CMO has presented a reasonable-looking plan that asks for a marketing spend of $1 million to achieve this 30 percent growth in sales.

Is this an ROI of 300 percent (spend $1 million to get $3 million of incremental revenue)?

Or is it an ROI of 100 percent (spend $1 million to get $1 million of incremental contribution margin)?

Or is it an ROI of 0 percent, since you are left with zero incremental dollars in the bottom line, after spending every dollar of incremental contribution margin on your marketing?

The second issue with this approach is that it treats the impact of marketing as a one-time event. Even an average marketing program has an impact that lasts more than one lifecycle. Existing customers drive future revenue growth, either from their own repurchase or their influence on other buyers. How do you account for that? By not accounting for customer lifetime value (CLV), and abdicating your decision-making authority to a spreadsheet, you are probably making suboptimal decisions.

The third issue with this approach is that, even if ROI is calculated and used correctly, maximizing ROI will not maximize sales or profit. Yes, you read that correctly. Maximizing ROI is not the same as maximizing your sales or profit opportunity.

This is due to the law of diminishing returns. In most instances, the first dollar you spend on advertising will have a much greater impact than the second or the third dollar. In other words, with every dollar you spend, you will get less bang for that buck, reducing your ROI each time you add a dollar to your spend.

Thus, if you maximize ROI, your spreadsheet will want you to underspend your budget. However, you probably measure your success with sales or profit at the end of the year (or month or quarter). To maximize either of these, you will need to spend more than the level that maximizes ROI.

Fortunately, there are smart, progressive, and confident marketers out there, who understand the value and limitations of ROI and use it as a metric if (and only when) it makes sense. When he was consumer marketing director at Microsoft, Paul Davies explained that the company had moved beyond being "very attribution-based and backward-looking" in their marketing, to a "much more forward-looking questioning: 'What's the next thing coming?'"[12]

To be clear, when he refers to attribution, Davies is talking about ROI. So, if you're going to avoid becoming overly focused on ROI, how can you measure the success of marketing programs? As you will recall, I mentioned that Apple continues to support the use of billboards by measuring how many eyeballs get exposed to them, and for how long. Similarly, you can also use other relevant key metrics (e.g., page opens, landing-page visits, call-to-action responses) that can be tracked, over a period of time, and used to evaluate how well your marketing programs are working, even if you're unable to have any meaningful attribution of specific sales to those programs.

Unfortunately, this obsession with numbers doesn't start and end with just ROI. There is an overreliance on data in general.

To appreciate why this might be a problem, let's look at its genesis.

THE ORIGINS OF THE DATA/ROI OBSESSIONS

It wasn't so long ago that marketers, and business leaders in general, didn't really have a way to gather direct data about their marketing efforts. Indeed, until just a few decades ago, companies had very little access to data across the board. Products were made by a factory, then distributed by a distributor, then sold to a dealer or retailer, and then sold to customers.

Beyond that first link in the chain, the company had little visibility into what happened along the way. They tried to gain some visibility, of course, but the limits of technology ensured that large gaps were always present. Leaders were desperate to peer into the gaps.

And then, beginning just a few decades ago, technology

began providing ways to collect data. Suddenly, companies could track things like card swipes, online clicks, and so on. It was exciting! Because of all the pent-up hunger for data, companies began investing heavily in acquiring and collecting any and all data they could possibly get. It has now come to a point where companies are spending time and money collecting far more data than they can ever use in a meaningful way. "Collect it, and we will find a use for it" is the modern-day, digital version of, "If you build it, they will come."

Today, companies have access to more data than ever, on just about anything you can imagine. Every customer interaction or activity can be tracked at a granular level. Even if there's no real or imminent use for most of this data, companies are still investing in acquiring it and storing it all in the cloud, as the marginal cost to store incremental data has become relatively trivial.

I believe marketers and business leaders would be far better served figuring out what to do with the data before they collect it, rather than just trying to collect more and more of it. Debra Bass, former president of Johnson & Johnson, has called this overabundance of data "infobesity." The term is apt. Marketers are gorging on data which, instead of giving them agility over competition, is leaving them lethargic and dazed, just as one feels after overeating.

Let's look at an illustrative analogy. A car is very useful for getting you where you want to go. However, when you put too many of them on the highway and fail to manage the flow, you get a traffic jam. If it's bad enough, you wind up with gridlock. The net effect is that nobody gets where they want to go quickly. The same can be said for overabundance of data when you don't manage its flow or usefulness.

One of the reasons for this ever-increasing problem is that data in the hands of a marketer is like candy in the hands of a child. They never have enough to satisfy the craving. Filling terabytes of cloud storage with granular data does nothing by itself.

I understand the temptation, but I strongly encourage businesses to pause, take a step back, and consider why they are collecting data in the first place. Take a more purposeful approach to data. Instead of just collecting as much information as possible, use your own business objectives to identify the pieces of information that are critical. Then figure out how and where you can acquire this specific information. Once you know which data to collect, why you're collecting it, and where you can find it, come up with an effective, ethical methodology and tool(s) for acquiring it.

We've become too reliant on only data. Instead of using data to inform their judgment and decision-making, marketers have started to hide behind it. They waste a vast amount of time and effort acquiring data to shield them from the responsibility and consequences of making smart decisions.

So how did this obsession with ROI begin?

I believe its roots come from the fact that marketers had to sit around the same table as engineers and compete for their budget dollars, using the tools and metrics that were already established and working well for those engineers. It's relatively easy and accurate to represent the cost of setting up a new manufacturing plant, and its expected output over time. All of this feeds smoothly into an ROI calculation. But how do you translate the effect of a billboard on incremental sales? How do you measure the confidence your potential customers gain by seeing you at a trade show even if they never give you purchase orders at that trade show?

I want to make it clear that I'm not opposed to ROI. When it can be reasonably connected to a campaign, ROI is great. However, sometimes you have to pursue that right-brain intuition in your marketing, creating and promoting the vision and message of your company in ways that might not be so easy to measure. Indeed, if you insist on attaching clear ROI to everything your marketing team does, you're going to miss out on some really effective and creative ways to build brand visibility.

Don't look for data just to hide behind it. Don't force an ROI number into a marketing campaign. Focus on your objectives, messaging, and positioning; trust the experience, intuition, and intelligence of your marketing team. And don't be afraid to get a little creative. That's how brands like Apple have created such loyal fans. Keep in mind that the maxim often attributed to Einstein—"Not everything that counts can be counted"—applies very well in the world of marketing.

Let me close this chapter with a pithy saying I first heard from my statistics professor. He was well grounded in the power and limitations of statistics, and he made sure we understood that statistics are often "like a lamppost to a drunk man: more for support and less for light."

CHAPTER FIFTEEN

READY, FIRE, AIM

If you are a naval gunner, you might look at the title of this chapter and be reminded of exactly what you were taught to do: ready your weapon, then fire a shot. If the first shot went too far, you'll adjust the gun and fire your second shot a little closer. If the second shot fell short, now you know exactly where to aim to hit the target dead-on.

This approach works under two conditions. One, you have more than enough ammo. Two, you are fairly confident that your target is not going to either escape or, worse, fire back at you, more accurately, before you have a chance to take them out.

Unfortunately, in most business situations, these two conditions are usually not present. Businesses are almost always resource-constrained; and very few competitors will sit idly by as you fine-tune your aim at them. Thus, you must avoid putting the proverbial cart before the horse and take aim before you fire.

TACTICS BEFORE STRATEGY?

RUSH, RUSH, MISS!

Let's look at some examples and see if we can learn from others' mistakes. Even some big, successful companies fired too soon, only to miss their target...and they've paid a hefty price for it.

Google is infamously guilty of firing too soon, before taking aim. In 2013, the company's line of smart glasses, Google Glass, hit the market with the expected level of fanfare and high expectations from the media pundits. But customer response ran the gamut from confusion over the device's purpose to outright hostility over privacy concerns. Surely, if Google had taken their time with the product and done enough customer research, they would have realized that this strange device was going to miss the mark.

The privacy concerns alone should have made Google take a step back and reconsider the messaging and positioning of their new product. Instead, Google rushed out a product they thought would establish them as a viable producer of cool gadgets, much like Apple.

Electric cars are all the rage these days, but did you know General Motors launched an electric vehicle back in 1996? The General Motors EV1 was the first mass-produced electric car from a major auto manufacturer in the modern era. But, surprisingly, it was only available to consumers in just two states: California and Arizona. As it turned out, the vehicle couldn't handle a cooler climate, which greatly limited its usability across the nation.

Reducing its chances of success even further, the vehicle was launched without any reasonable infrastructure in place to support customers. There were practically no charging facilities, and the vehicle's initial range was under a hundred miles. It was a cool-sounding idea that ultimately missed its target, and within three years, GM shut it down.

If you're old enough, you might remember the war between VHS and Betamax video recorders.

Betamax was a higher-quality product, but the tapes were limited to recording only one hour. Of course, most movies run at least ninety minutes (and Bollywood movies often run nearly twice as long). Somehow, Sony didn't do even the simplest of research to realize that this obvious limitation was going to kill them in the market.

You might also remember, or have heard of, the New Coke debacle in 1985, when Coca-Cola made the ill-advised decision to change the recipe of their flagship product, despite the fact that customers weren't clamoring for a change. It seems they launched New Coke just to make waves, but it backfired spectacularly on them.

According to polls, only 13 percent of soda drinkers liked the new recipe. The company received tens of thousands of complaint letters, and a disgruntled customer even created a protest group called Old Cola Drinkers of America. Within three months, they reintroduced the original Coke formula, rebranding it Coca-Cola Classic, but the cautionary tale lives on forever![13]

Ready, fire, aim, and miss.

SLOW DOWN AND TAKE AIM

Business leaders, and especially CEOs, are keen to execute. As the oft-heard expression goes, "It's all about execution." They want to hit the market fast, beat the competition onto the shelves, and get the word out before people even know what hit them. This puts pressure on the rest of the company to rush products, services, advertisements, and just about everything else.

We all want to beat the competition to the market, and that temptation makes it very hard not to pull the trigger. But this mindset of needing something yesterday only encourages fast actions—not necessarily well-aimed ones.

My advice is to slow down a little bit. Take a deep breath. Make sure you're aiming at the right target—and aiming well. It's better to take some extra time, to make sure your hasty decision isn't going to damage your brand or waste precious resources. When you're ready, take the time to aim, and then—and only then—pull the trigger.

Chapter Sixteen

CRACKING THE GOOGLE CODE

During my time as a corporate CMO, I constantly received emails from SEO marketing companies. They were usually worded as helpful warnings that Google had, once again, changed its algorithm, followed by a well-intended and timely suggestion for me to consider revising our website. Not surprisingly, the sender typically provided details about how their company was best positioned to help me with this.

Countless marketing companies are trying to get people to purchase their services, with the promise of gaming the latest changes in Google's algorithm. There are a couple of things to know about this. First, it's true that Google revises its search algorithm frequently; in fact, far more frequently than these marketing companies can keep up with. Second, Google is extremely secretive about their algorithm, so there's little chance that most of these self-professed SEO experts can actually help anyone "game the system."

The good news is you don't need to crack the Google code to win with Google.

When it comes to their search engine, Google has clear objectives, which they reveal openly and clearly on their website.

In explaining their search-engine algorithm, Google provides some basic advice to webmasters for rising in Google search rankings. On their website, they state:

- Make pages primarily for users, not for search engines.
- Don't deceive your users.
- Avoid tricks intended to improve search engine rankings. A good rule of thumb is whether you'd feel comfortable explaining what you have done, to a website that competes with you, or to a Google employee. Another useful test is to ask, "Does this help my users? Would I do this if search engines didn't exist?"
- Think about what makes your website unique, valuable, or engaging. Make your website stand out from others in your field.[14]

These four principles provide the necessary and sufficient advice for webmasters who want to rise in the search rankings. Beyond this, there's no trick, secret technique, or magical formula for tricking Google into pushing your website higher in the search results. Companies that promise they can help you do this are mostly making empty promises.

J.C. PENNEY IN THE DOGHOUSE

Attempting to game the system is a good way to waste money. Unfortunately, a lot of unscrupulous SEO companies are all too eager to help you do it. Even if they somehow manage to succeed in boosting your website a few ranks in the search engine, you run the risk of getting into trouble. If Google realizes what you're doing, they will penalize you.

In 2011, J.C. Penney tried to run a link-building scheme to juice their Google ranking. Essentially, they were paying money to get thousands of unrelated websites to link back to JCPenney.com. Google realized something was up when the website suddenly surged up in organic search results. They promptly investigated and discovered the scam.

When J.C. Penney was confronted about this, they claimed ignorance and placed the blame on an SEO firm they'd hired. However, the damage was done. Google forced J.C. Penney to remove the phony links, and the company dropped drastically in the rankings.

PURSUE RELEVANCE, NOT TRICKS

Google is not the enemy. They're not trying to stop you from being successful; they just want to serve users by providing the most relevant search results. If you think about it, that's your job as well—serving your customers. Thus, if you design a website that serves your customers well, Google will notice and reward you for it.

View Google and other search engines as partners in your effort to reach people, not as obstacles to overcome by any means possible. Everything you need to know about Google's search algorithm is right there on their website, for everyone to see. Despite what you may be told to the contrary, there's no trick to it.

It's true that your website might need a refresh. However, the reason is not because of some recent change to Google's algorithm. Instead, your website might benefit from changes that make it more customer-focused and easier to navigate, providing useful information to customers more quickly and simply. Your users should be the inspiration for change, not Google's algorithm.

CHAPTER SEVENTEEN

MONKEY BUSINESS WITH LONG TAILS

I still remember my first meeting with a proud CEO who hired my company Chief Outsiders to help with marketing initiatives. He seemed incredibly excited, boasting about how his company's website had risen in Google search results. Over the previous six months, he said, they had crawled their way from page five or six to the first page, by purchasing some search engine optimization.

To be honest, my first thought was, "Then what am I doing here?" They'd spent money on SEO and got the results they wanted, so why had they hired me? I began probing the issue.

"So, you now rank within the top ten on relevant searches,"

I said. "What impact has that made on lead generation? Are you getting more prospective customers now?"

As it turned out, there was almost no correlation between the company's higher search engine rank on selective keywords and phrases and their lead generation. Indeed, in terms of sales, the company wasn't doing much better. When I dug a little deeper, I finally discovered the problem.

The company had climbed in search engine rankings by using long keyword phrases with very specific terms. In fact, the phrases they'd used were so long and esoteric that it was unlikely any real potential customer would ever search for them. Consequently, the higher ranking was essentially useless when it came to actual leads from real prospects.

Let's suppose you're an independent handyman with a website. Potential customers are far more likely to search for "handyman to repair drywall" than something overly specific like "handyman with a purple pickup truck," even if you drive a uniquely purple truck. Yes, you can easily rise in the rankings for the second phrase, but it's unlikely to do you any good in terms of actual sales.

That is what this company had done. They'd chosen some very specific phrases, which made it easy to rise in the rankings if and when those specific search phrases were used. However, it made no meaningful impact on lead generation or sales. It gave them a false sense of accomplishment, because what's the use of being number one if you're number one for phrases that are not being queried by real prospects?

I understand why companies do this. Paying an SEO company to boost you to the first page of search results for a common phrase is typically very expensive, because there's a lot of competition with other websites. On the other hand, it's relatively inexpensive to pay someone to boost your rank on some long, highly specific phrases.

This is such a common tactic that there's a term for these long and too-specific search terms: longtail phrases. Yes, hiring an SEO company to do some monkey business on a longtail phrase is likely to get you higher in the rankings, and that will feel good, but this ranking is meaningless if it doesn't impact your business.

WHERE'D THESE LONG TAILS COME FROM?

The long-tail concept was introduced to the business world by Chris Anderson, editor of Wired magazine, who, in 2006, wrote a book called The Long Tail: Why the Future of Business Is Selling Less of More. His primary thesis was that businesses can make a lot of money if they focus on something other people aren't focusing on.

As he explained, consumers can now go online to find products tailored to very specific tastes, so smart online businesses should start focusing on niche offerings, instead of fighting for dominance amongst a lot of competition. He created a well-known graph to illustrate this point, which is the origin of the term long-tail. Aim for the tail, he suggested, where unique products are found, rather than the head, where competition is fierce.

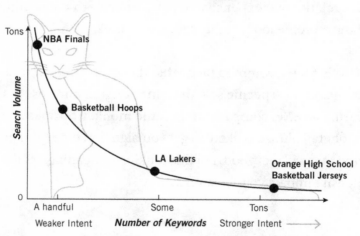

SEO: PRIME WORDS VS LONG-TAIL PHRASES

It's the difference between people searching for "NBA finals" and "orange high school basketball jerseys." Plenty of people will search for the first phrase, making competition fierce; relatively few will search for the latter, creating a niche that a company might fill. In terms of search rankings, it's going to be a lot cheaper to climb to the first page with "orange high school basketball jerseys." That's where the longtail temptation comes into play.

As a CEO or business leader, however, I ask you to consider your company's primary objective in using longtail search SEO. Your primary goal is not to save money but to make money. This goal should drive your SEO plan.

So, is Chris Anderson wrong? No. Finding a niche can be lucrative. However, if you aim too small, you might wind up in a niche with no customers in it. Instead, a good marketer will use a combination of longtail phrases with a few common terms, striking the right balance between visibility and specificity.

Another way to find the sweet spot between expensive search terms and inexpensive long-tail phrases is to ask yourself what your goal is. If you're looking to build awareness, stay closer to general terms that people are likely to search for, even if they are more expensive. If you're already well-known and are now looking to impact your conversion rate, you could lean more toward using long-tail phrases to draw people who are aware of your company to parts of the website that are new and might be relevant to those long-tail phrases.

To put it simply, common terms will create more awareness of your brand, by reaching a broad swath of potential customers. Long-tail phrases are handy if you are seeking to boost engagement among prospects who already know you.

Another possible approach, which is called hypertargeting, uses different landing pages for each of your rare search terms. Even if you only get one or two searches for a specific longtail phrase, each month, having a landing page tailored to that phrase almost guarantees that your content will be very relevant to anyone who finds their way there. Visitors will only arrive infrequently, but when they do, they will almost always be highly engaged.

MYTHS ABOUT LONG TAILS

There are some myths about longtail phrases that I frequently encounter when I talk to business leaders.

First, many leaders assume that using longtail phrases alone is enough to dominate a niche and grow your business. This almost never works. You have to use them in combination with a few commonly searched terms. Otherwise, you won't get enough meaningful traffic to grow your business.

Second, many leaders believe that focusing solely on longtail phrases is cost-effective and saves money. While it's certainly cheaper to boost rankings using longtail phrases, you're probably not going to make enough money to make it worthwhile. After all, isn't it really about getting more customers? If you fail to do that, then what's the point of spending any money?

Third, many business leaders seem to think that the longer a phrase is, the better. However, a really long phrase is going to become so rare that it might never be searched by anyone. A good rule of thumb is to limit long-tail phrases to three or four words. People rarely search for phrases longer than that.

Strike the right balance, based on your specific objectives. Don't fall for any monkey business with long tails without fully understanding the implications.

CHAPTER EIGHTEEN

LET'S AUTOMATE

Garbage in, garbage out. It's a saying that, I'm afraid, applies well to all business processes.

One of the most common mistakes in sales and marketing is to automate processes without first fixing them. If you automate a garbage process, you will only get automated garbage faster! This is a particular problem with customer relationship management (CRM) software.

A wide range of vendors offer CRM platforms with various capabilities and price points, but in general, they come in three flavors:

1. CRM platforms focused on sales, which include sales force automation tools

2. CRM platforms focused on marketing, which include marketing automation tools
3. CRM platforms focused on both sales and marketing

In my experience, for most companies, the best choice comes from the third category.

When a small company begins to grow, at some point the CEO will read or hear about the power of automation. Indeed, it's practically a buzzword when it comes to CRM. The CEO of that growing company gets excited about the possibilities of automation and rushes to implement it. This is not inherently a bad thing, but some common mistakes are often made at this point.

Let's look at some of these mistakes and also see what you can do to avoid them. I have arranged them, not in order of importance or significance, but in chronological order, as you will likely encounter them in your automation journey.

- Perpetuating Process Flaws. This is where "garbage in, garbage out" comes into play. If you have a broken marketing process and you automate it, you'll simply produce garbage even faster and more consistently.
- Overinvesting in Your CRM. Customer relationship management platforms come in a range of price points, from the more robust, expensive solution, full of bells and whistles, provided by Salesforce, to a vari-

ety of smaller CRMs. Sometimes business leaders are entranced by all of the shiny features provided by an expensive, fully featured CRM platform, and they end up spending a lot more than they should for nonessential features that they don't need. Perhaps including a few potential users of your CRM would help you to select a better platform, with features that your employees will embrace.

- Losing Your Uniqueness. Your company might have some unique characteristics in the way you approach and interact with customers, but many of the popular CRM platforms over-standardize. Inadvertently, the platform might force you to lose your valuable uniqueness. This typically happens when companies assume bigger is better. They spend more for a popular platform, rather than finding a CRM that best meets their specific needs today and in the foreseeable future.

- New Tool, No Mastery. In Chapter Eleven, we talked about the danger of adopting tools but failing to train your organization to work with them. The same can happen with a CRM platform. It won't do you much good to buy a nice, new CRM platform if you don't invest the time and money in training your people to make the most of it.

- Failure to Update Processes. Once you've implemented a CRM, you have to keep your processes updated, as conditions change in your industry and market, or as a result of global/national events. For example, consider the way successful companies had to adjust their processes to deal with COVID-19 lockdowns and social distancing. Both the software itself and your processes need to be regularly updated as situations evolve around you. Many companies find themselves struggling with their CRM because outdated processes no longer meet their current needs.

- Using CRM to Stalk Customers. Customer interactions are the lifeblood of any organization. However, the way you deal with your customers can make either a positive or negative impact. A common mistake companies make with their CRM platform is to stalk customers instead of attracting and serving them. It's easy to fall into this habit, because you can send 10,000 emails to your mailing list with the press of a button. You can also digitally stalk them by responding to every little move your potential customers make on your website. Yes, a CRM platform provides the power to stalk customers, but that doesn't mean you should do it. As useful as a good CRM platform can be, it also makes it easy to annoy customers. Resist the temptation for your own sake (if not for your customers' peace of mind).

MAKING THE MOST OF CRM

It may be small comfort, but the truth is that even large, successful organizations have made some of the CRM mistakes discussed in this chapter. So, if you're making some of them yourself, you're in good company. The most famous example is Hershey's Chocolate Company's catastrophic enterprise resource planning (ERP) software implementation failure, in 1999. The company wanted to upgrade their legacy IT systems, so they invested $112 million in what was then a cutting-edge system, to manage their supply chain and customer relationships.

The software went live during Hershey's busiest time of the year, at the end of the summer, when they normally receive the bulk of their Halloween candy orders from retailers. However, their implementation team had rushed, cut corners, and failed to properly test and implement correct processes. As a result, the company was unable to process around $100 million in candy orders.

In my estimation, a big part of the problem was that Hershey selected a platform with a lot of bells and whistles they didn't need.

They over-invested in cutting-edge software, then rushed implementation and launched it, at the worst possible time, with the greatest risk of failure and cost associated with it. Their team was ill-prepared and undertrained, processes weren't refined, and they paid a massive price for this failure, which could have been easily mitigated or avoided altogether.

Customer relationship management software provides

some powerful tools for more effectively reaching your target audience and meeting the needs of your customers. However, it's easy to make some of these common mistakes and turn a useful tool into a hindrance. Consider carefully how you are using your CRM software to ensure you're getting the most out of it for your organization.

CHAPTER NINETEEN

SELF BEFORE SERVICE

A school I attended as a child had the motto service before self. It's also the motto of the US Air Force and the Indian Army. But you don't have to be associated with any of the aforementioned institutions to intuitively understand the value of this dictum. Most of us try to live up to this in our lives. When you hire a marketing services company, it's only reasonable to expect to receive service before any self-serving motives.

Unfortunately, far too often, we experience self before service instead.

As you may have noticed, there are many (arguably, far too many) consultants, agencies, and businesses that claim to provide marketing services. According to data compiled by IBIS World in 2020, in the United States, there were approximately:

- 75,000 ad agencies
- 21,000 digital ad agencies
- 40,000 market research companies
- 46,000 PR firms
- 92,000 SEO and internet marketing specialists
- 75,000 web design companies/specialists
- 226,000 marketing consultants[15]

Granted, there is likely some double counting, as many service providers legitimately provide more than one service. Still, it's safe to assume that the number of choices available to anyone searching for the generic term of marketing runs into a few hundred thousand. It could be as high as half a million!

With so many choices, you should be able to find the perfect match, right?

In theory, yes. But it gets murky very fast.

As you may have noticed, I am a big believer in getting the strategy right before jumping to the execution of tactics. When you start your search for the perfect marketing services provider, you will quickly discover that almost every one of them claims to provide you with strategy.

The problem with such claims is that they are almost always incorrect and are largely self-serving.

It's no secret that marketing is a big word (remember the parable about the elephant and the five blind men). It includes knowing what product features your customers want. It also includes knowing how to price your products and services. Understanding which channels you should be using to reach to your target audience is a part of marketing, as is segmentation and positioning for each of the chosen segments. Then you get to decide what your message should be, so that it will resonate with your target audience.

Speaking of messaging, today you have a multitude of traditional and digital channels to get your word out. All of these are well within the scope of marketing. What about market research? Check! And PR? Check! Customer satisfaction, and how it might influence future sales? Check, check, check!

All of the above (and more) reside comfortably together under the big tent we call marketing.

To be capable of taking a truly holistic view and developing a comprehensive strategy that works for you and your specific situation (and isn't a cut-and-paste from an old Harvard Business Review article or another client's deck), you need decades of hands-on experience doing all of the things mentioned above. It is highly unlikely that a specialist in any field can legitimately claim to have this kind of capability.

So when your SEO vendor claims to do marketing strategy, it's entirely possible that they mean they will create a strategic-sounding document that will steer you toward—you guessed it—SEO! When you talk to a website development company, their strategic document will—surprise, surprise—recommend developing a new website.

You get the point. To a hammer, everything is a nail. Every marketing specialist is going to develop a strategy that steers you toward the specific services they provide. This is self before service, in full action, right in front of your eyes.

So, what can you do to circumvent this pervasive problem?

First of all, being aware that this is a problem in the first place is a very good start. With this in mind, ask deeper questions that might challenge the specialist beyond their stated expertise, to see if they truly are capable of a higher-level strategic perspective on marketing. Are they too deeply focused on their own specialization? Can they draw a big picture relating their area of expertise to something that is entirely unrelated but would be part of your overall strategy?

There's nothing wrong with seeking a specialist, but don't expect the specialist to give you an effective overall strategy for your business, just as you wouldn't go to an orthopedic surgeon who specializes in shoulders for an overall assessment of your health.

Second, if you don't have a senior-level, experienced marketer on your leadership team, consider hiring a fractional or an interim C-level marketer to develop and manage your strategy. They can help you convert your strategy into effective tactics that deliver results.

Third, look for a senior-level professional who doesn't have a personal vested interest in any of the specialist marketing vendors. You want to get unbiased advice and recommendations. Just as you don't expect any of your employees to make business decisions that are influenced by self-interest, you should hold your outside vendors and partners to the same standard.

Watch for and weed out self-serving marketing providers who overstate their abilities and claim to take a holistic view of your business situation, without any credibility or experience to back it. Instead, look for an experienced marketing professional who has the years and scars to take a holistic approach and has only your interests in mind when making any recommendations.

You deserve service before self, and you should demand it.

CONCLUSION

If you came to this book, full of frustration at the lack of results you've been getting for your marketing spend, know that you are not alone. In my lifelong career in marketing, I have seen more than my fair share of marketing shenanigans that are nothing short of "lies and damned lies."

My goal has been to strip away much of the confusion and misguided thinking that leads to such disappointing results. The tips and techniques I have shared in the preceding chapters are meant to provide the insights you need to rise above the frustration, avoid these "lies and damned lies," and do real, effective marketing with confidence.

Remember, marketing is about the future and making tactical decisions to reach potential customers down the road. Start with your Big-M marketing, the foundational elements that help define your business strategy—a foundation based on rich insights from your customers and a solid understanding of the competitive landscape, as well as your own company, team, and capabilities. Once you've laid a strong foundation, you can begin implementing your small-m marketing tactics in order to move the needle and deliver business growth.

I've shown some effective ways to do both of these. Keep in mind, it's not just about doing the right things, but also doing them in the right order (Big-M strategic stuff before small-m tactics). Appeal to the left brain and the right brain, with an awareness of the cognitive biases that influence customer decisions. This will help you choose the right media, using both digital and traditional marketing channels. Any time you need to know more about your customers, think of how you might have rich, engaging conversations with key customers and partners.

We also discussed the importance of creating an active—but real and authentic—fan base on social media and examined ways to master your marketing technology tools, improve your tactics, and unify your marketing efforts toward clear objectives.

And in the last chapter, I exposed an all-too-common trick most marketing agencies play by offering to do your "strategic plan," that is more self-serving than serving your (or your customers') best interests.

DO I NEED MARKETING?

I really hope you are not asking this question. But, in case you still are, let me remind you of the chart I showed you in the introduction of this book: the top ten reasons why companies fail. Let's take a look at it again.

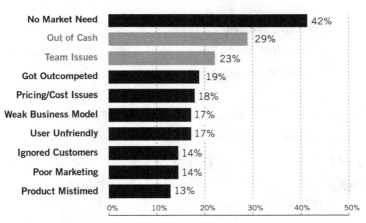

8 OUT OF TOP 10 REASONS FOR FAILURE CAN BE AVOIDED WITH GOOD MARKETING

Reason	Percentage
No Market Need	42%
Out of Cash	29%
Team Issues	23%
Got Outcompeted	19%
Pricing/Cost Issues	18%
Weak Business Model	17%
User Unfriendly	17%
Ignored Customers	14%
Poor Marketing	14%
Product Mistimed	13%

Source: CB Insights, Nov 2019.

As the chart shows clearly, effective and timely marketing will fix eight out of ten of these problems. So, just think about how marketing can drive the growth of your business once you've patched the holes in your strategy and successfully avoided all of the "lies and damned lies."

Are you getting excited about the possibilities?

You should be. The truth is, you have an amazing array of

marketing opportunities at your fingertips, just waiting to be put into action for maximum advantage.

As you read through this book, certain chapters or topics may have stood out, as you identified particular areas of frustration or specific struggles you're currently dealing with. Now that you've finished the book, let me encourage you to go back and refer to those topics, so you can begin to strategize and put some amazing, effective solutions into action. You may be on the cusp of a remarkable transformation in your marketing strategy.

To make this easier for you, I have included a simple, topical outline of every chapter, after the conclusion. However, if you're looking for more help with your marketing strategy or tactics, or if you'd like to contact me, please see my contact information at the end of this book.

REFERENCE GUIDE

Following is a brief summary of the major points included in each of this book's chapters. My purpose is to provide an easy way to find the most relevant topics for your business, so you can begin to implement impactful changes to your marketing. This will also make it easier to find specific sections of the book that are of the most interest to you.

PART ONE: WHAT IS MARKETING?
CHAPTER ONE: LET'S DEFINE MARKETING

- Sales is focused on the present, while marketing is focused on the future.
- Big-M Marketing: a strategy that sets the stage, revealing a path that will get you to a better place in the future.
- Small-m Marketing: the tactics you can implement to move the needle right now.

- Great marketing always places the ultimate customer at the center of everything.

PART TWO: BIG-M MARKETING
CHAPTER TWO: LEFT BRAIN OR RIGHT BRAIN

- Marketers have to appeal to both the left brain (data) and right brain (emotion) to engage customers and make them pay attention.
- Start with the right brain before delivering data to the left brain.

CHAPTER THREE: BEING RATIONAL ABOUT IRRATIONALITY

- Humans are prone to irrational decisions, because of cognitive biases.
- People prefer a small reward now over a greater reward in the future.
- Learn to recognize cognitive biases, so you can predict how potential customers will respond to your messaging.

CHAPTER FOUR: RICHES ARE IN NICHES...BUT NOT IN TRENCHES

- It is a huge mistake to specialize in a single vertical or industry, especially when you're just starting out. You will hinder your future growth.

- Focus on what's unique about you that attracts customers to your products and services.

CHAPTER FIVE: IT'S ALL DIGITAL NOW

- "Digital" is simply a medium—one of many—that can and should be used for marketing.
- You have to find creative ways to stand out, and if you only focus on digital marketing, you'll have to work extra hard to do that.
- At each step of the customer journey, consider how your target audience is consuming information, and use the most appropriate medium—digital or traditional—to reach them.

CHAPTER SIX: YES, OUR CFO MANAGES PRICING

- The leader who is given control over pricing will make decisions according to their own role in the company. The best person to do this is neither your CFO nor your VP of Sales.
- You have to go beyond the math, beyond the profit margin, to look at the psychology of pricing.
- Your CMO is best suited to make strategic decisions about pricing.

CHAPTER SEVEN: SPEED (ALONE) KILLS

- Most CEOs like to move fast, but customers don't necessarily or always care which company is first to market.
- I recommend velocity over speed, moving at the right speed but also in the right direction.

CHAPTER EIGHT: QUANTITY OVER QUALITY (IN RESEARCH)

- When it comes to customer insight, quality matters more than quantity.
- Focus on having a few rich, engaging conversations with individuals in your target audience.

PART THREE: SMALL-M MARKETING

CHAPTER NINE: SOCIAL DISTANCING IN SOCIAL MEDIA

- Dumping a bunch of marketing content onto social media, without the right positioning and messaging, might be a complete waste of time and money.
- Social media marketing requires careful consideration and smart planning. It's not a silver bullet.

CHAPTER TEN: LIKES AND FOLLOWERS

- The only person who profits when you pay for fake likes

and followers is the guy running the shady company that provides them.

- A small, active but real fan base is more effective than a vast sea of faceless followers who never speak.

CHAPTER ELEVEN: MORE TOOLS, LESS MASTERY

- When it comes to choosing marketing technology tools for your company, don't chase after the shiniest new tool.
- Look for established tools that have gone through the crescendo of hype and come out the other side intact.
- Make sure your company is prepared to invest the time and money in training employees to use your new tool.

CHAPTER TWELVE: QUANTITY OVER QUALITY (IN TACTICS)

- If you're not getting good results from your marketing efforts, you probably don't need more tactics; you need better tactics.
- Do less marketing. Focus on creating higher-quality marketing content rather than trying to do as much as possible.

CHAPTER THIRTEEN: RANDOM ACTS OF MARKETING

- Even if your individual marketing efforts are being done

skillfully, you still need to coordinate them all, so they work well together.

- When your marketing efforts aren't coordinated, it becomes very difficult to tell which ones are working and which ones aren't.

- Spend some time creating a strategic marketing plan before you get into specific marketing tactics.

PART FOUR: BIG-M + SMALL-M MARKETING

CHAPTER FOURTEEN: FAKE ROI

- If you insist on attaching ROI to everything your marketing team does, you're going to miss out on some effective ways to build your brand visibility.

- Business leaders would be far better served figuring out what to do with their data before collecting more and more of it.

CHAPTER FIFTEEN: READY, FIRE, AIM

- The attitude that says, "I need this yesterday," only encourages fast (shotgun) actions over well-aimed actions.

- Make sure you are aiming at the right target—and aiming well. It's better to take some extra time to make sure your haste isn't going to damage your brand.

CHAPTER SIXTEEN: CRACKING THE GOOGLE CODE

- You don't need to crack the Google code to win with Google.
- Attempting to game the system is a good way to waste money, and you run the risk of getting into trouble.
- Focus on your customers and strive to serve them well. Google will reward you for doing so.

CHAPTER SEVENTEEN: MONKEY BUSINESS WITH LONG TAILS

- Using SEO on long-tail phrases is liable to get you high in the rankings, but it's meaningless if nobody's searching for your too-specific terms.
- A good marketer will use a combination of long-tail phrases with a few common terms, striking the right balance between visibility and specificity.

CHAPTER EIGHTEEN: LET'S AUTOMATE

- If you have a broken marketing process and you automate it, you'll simply produce garbage even faster and more consistently.
- Fix the process first, then consider automating it.

CHAPTER NINETEEN: SELF BEFORE SERVICE

- To a hammer, everything looks like a nail. There are

many specialists who focus on specific tactics, and many of them will claim to offer marketing strategy. However, they will invariably push you toward the tactics that they specialize in.

- If you're going to hire someone to help with your marketing strategy, look for an experienced marketing professional who can take a holistic approach, with no personal or vested interest in making recommendations.

ACKNOWLEDGMENTS

This book and, quite frankly my entire career, would not have come together if not for all of the managers who displayed confidence in me and my abilities, well beyond what I thought I had.

From the late Mr. T.G. Kripalani, the first CEO of Toyota's India project, who "dragged" me into marketing, to Kate Sandweiss at Cummins, who had the instinct to hire me as her marketing manager for Europe (even though I had never been to Europe) because she believed that my upbringing in a diverse country like India would make me sensitive to, and respectful of, the diversity of Europe—I owe them all deepest thanks.

Building on this early success in marketing, I was lucky to cross paths with Regina (Pizzoli) Sutton and Rick Cimino, both of whom took a chance to hire me at Kodak Health Imaging, even though I had no experience in healthcare marketing. "We will give you time to learn the industry, as long as you come prepared to share your marketing prowess and creativity," is how they put it when they made the job offer. This migration from automotive/industrial to healthcare further fed my innate curiosity and thirst for learning new lines of business and industries.

I also want to acknowledge my colleagues and managers at Honeywell, Graco, Smith & Nephew, and Covance, who all shaped my marketing thinking and prepared me for my next career chapter of consulting in marketing.

Art Saxby and Pete Hayes, co-founders of Chief Outsiders, never tire of saying that they created the firm to be a place where former CMOs of Fortune 1000 companies can come to do their best work in the service of driving growth at emerging and midsize companies. I want to thank both of them for bringing me into the partnership early in the firm's evolution. I can't thank my colleagues and clients enough for continuing to give me opportunities to learn and practice the craft of marketing.

I also want to thank over a thousand students I have had the privilege of teaching since 2009. They may not have realized this, but I have learned as much from them as they have from me. As they fed their own curiosity and hunger for marketing knowledge, they kept me current in the field of marketing. No formal education program could have given me as wide an exposure to marketing practices around the world as these students have by participating and engaging in active class discussions. My heartfelt thanks to all of them!

And finally, I want to thank the good folks who worked diligently to bring this book to life. While I am sure there are numerous people at Lioncrest Publishing who have their fingerprints all over this book, I am especially grateful for the significant contributions of Natalie Aboudaoud, Rachel Brandenburg, Alexa Davis, Jeffrey Miller, Nikki Van Noy, Miles Rote, and their teams.

And while my colleague, friend, and cheerful admirer of everything Mark Twain, Professor A.C. Ross, is not part of the team at Lioncrest (as far as I can tell), I owe him a deep debt of gratitude for suggesting the title of this book. His quick wit and generosity in sharing his knowledge is admirable. Our discussions over the years have helped crystalize my own thinking on all things marketing and data, some of which is reflected in this book.

ABOUT THE AUTHOR

ATUL MINOCHA'S professional life is centered within three slightly overlapping circles: consulting/mentoring, teaching, and investing in entrepreneurial ventures.

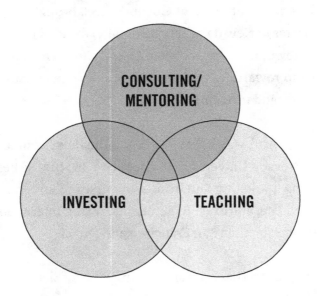

Atul arrived at the intersection of these circles by way of first getting a degree in mechanical engineering at the Indian Institute of Technology, Delhi, later discovering his passion for marketing upon starting his career at Toyota's India Project.

With this newfound passion for marketing, Atul decided to come to the United States to formalize his study of marketing by pursuing an MBA at Yale University. He rose through the ranks of marketing and product management roles at Cummins, Graco, and Honeywell, which led to CMO roles at Kodak Health Imaging and Smith & Nephew, and culminated in running Covance Cardiac Safety Services as general manager.

His last corporate role, at Covance CSS, brought him to the Sierras in Nevada, where he (finally) decided to put his roots down, in the shadows of Lake Tahoe. This opened new and rewarding opportunities for him in consulting, teaching, and investing.

In 2009, Atul was invited to teach business courses at Sierra Nevada University at Lake Tahoe. In 2013, he began teaching marketing and business courses to undergraduate, graduate, and executive students, at Hult International Business School, in San Francisco and Dubai.

Since 2010, Atul has been an active member of Sierra Angels, one of the pioneering angel groups outside of Silicon Valley. He serves on its executive and selection committees, and is also manager of their early-stage investment fund.

As a partner at Chief Outsiders, a national marketing firm he joined in 2012, Atul consults with growing and midsize companies in automotive, healthcare, industrial, software, and technology verticals.

When Atul is not living within the three circles above, he can be found feeding his curiosity and exploring the world on any of the seven continents. At the time of this book's publication, he had visited forty-seven countries and forty-nine states, federal districts, and territories of the United States.

Atul was born in Delhi, India, and has lived in the United States since 1987.

You can learn more about Atul and his professional interests and activities at atulminocha.com.

Feel free to connect with him on LinkedIn at linkedin.com/in/atulminocha.

NOTES

1   Fred Burt, "Steve Jobs Oldie but Goodie," YouTube Video, 6:54, Nov. 6, 2008, https://www.youtube.com/watch?v=vmG9jzCHtSQ%2012&ab_channel=FredBurt.

2   Andreas Hinterhuber, "Toward value-based pricing—An integrative framework for decision making," *Industrial Marketing Management* 33, no. 8 (November 2004): 765-778.

3   Julianne Pepitone, "Netflix loses 800,000 subscribers," *CNN Money*, Oct. 24, 2011, https://money.cnn.com/2011/10/24/technology/netflix_earnings/index.htm.

4   Motley Fool Staff, "Netflix, Inc. (NFLX) Q4 2017 Earnings Conference Call Transcript," Fool.com, Jan. 22, 2018, https://www.fool.com/earnings/call-transcripts/2018/01/22/netflix-inc-nflx-q4-2017-earnings-conference-call.aspx.

5   G. Suetonius Tranquillus, translated by Alexander Thomson, *The Lives of the Twelve Caesars, Complete* (2004), Project Gutenberg, http://www.gutenberg.org/ebooks/6400.

6   Charles Duhigg, "How Companies Learn Your Secrets," *The New York Times*, Feb. 19, 2012, https://www.nytimes.com/2012/02/19/magazine/shopping-habits.html.

7   Maggie Astor, "Dove Drops an Ad Accused of Racism," *New York Times*, Oct. 8, 2017, https://www.nytimes.com/2017/10/08/business/dove-ad-racist.html.

8   Hanna Ziady, "Volkswagen Apologized for Racist Ad," *CNN Business*, May 21, 2020, https://www.cnn.com/2020/05/21/business/volkswagen-racist-ad-instagram/index.html.

9   Hannah Ellis-Petersen, "Burger King removes 'racist' ad showing man trying to eat with giant chopsticks," *The Guardian*, April 9, 2019, https://www.theguardian.com/business/2019/apr/09/burger-king-removes-racist-ad-showing-man-trying-to-eat-with-giant-chopsticks.

10 Scott Brinker, "Marketing Technology Landscape Supergraphics (2020)," Chief Marketing Technologist Blog, April 22, 2020, https://chiefmartec.com/2020/04/marketing-technology-landscape-2020-martech-5000/.

11 "Waste or Win? The Case for Just-in-Time Marketing, by Accenture Interactive," *Accenture*, 2016, https://www.accenture.com/_acnmedia/pdf-18/accenture-waste-or-win-the-case-for-just-in-time-marketing-main2.pdf.

12 Sarah Vizard, "Marketers must beware of over-relying on ROI," *Marketing Week*, March 18, 2019, https://www.marketingweek.com/marketers-beware-over-rely-roi.

13 Rachid Haoues, "30 years ago today, Coca-Cola made its worst mistake," *CBS Evening News*, April 23, 2015, https://www.cbsnews.com/news/30-years-ago-today-coca-cola-new-coke-failure.

14 "Webmaster Guidelines," *Google Search Central*, last updated Dec. 8, 2020, https://developers.google.com/search/docs/advanced/guidelines/webmaster-guidelines.

15 IBISWorld, "Advertising Agencies in the US," IBISWorld Industry Report 54181, https://www.ibisworld.com/united-states/market-research-reports/advertising-agencies-industry/.

CPSIA information can be obtained
at www.ICGtesting.com
Printed in the USA
LVHW090020110821
695020LV00011B/146/J